8.95

DEAD AND GONE

DEAD AND GONE

CLASSIC CRIMES
OF NORTH CAROLINA

by

Manly Wade Wellman

Chapel Hill

THE UNIVERSITY OF NORTH CAROLINA PRESS

© 1954 The University of North Carolina Press
All rights reserved
Manufactured in the United States of America
Cloth edition, published 1954, ISBN 0-8078-0666-8
Paper edition, published 1980, ISBN 0-8078-4072-6
Library of Congress Catalog Card Number 55-391
92 91 90 89 88   9 8 7 6 5

To

Those Who Helped

FOREWORD

"PEOPLE BEGIN TO SEE," pronounces Thomas De Quincey in his lecture *On Murder Considered As One of the Fine Arts,* "that something more goes to the composition of a fine murder than two blockheads to kill and be killed—a knife—a purse—and a dark lane." Later in the same work, he develops the viewpoint: "Everything in this world has two handles. Murder, for instance, may be laid hold of by its moral handle (as it generally is in the pulpit, and at the Old Bailey) ; and *that,* I confess, is its weak side; or it may also be treated *aesthetically,* as the Germans call it—that is, in relation to good taste."

This attitude would have seemed curiously hyper-sophisticated to the forthright North Carolinians of the nineteenth century, when most of the events considered here took place. Yet these ten murders were each the object of tremendous and widespread interest among the masses of people, who, Tolstoi repeatedly assures us, are the critics most to be respected. Nor was this preoccupation due to any rarity of homicides there and then. For instance, from 1811 to 1815, North Carolina courts tried eighty-nine charges of murder, at a time when the state's population was less than 600,000, with only occasional small urban concentrations and no notable reputation for neuroses. Nor does that figure include manslaughters or unsuccessful attempts, or cases of escape from justice, or duels—frequent, those last, in an era of strong political rivalries, when statesmanship tended to walk hand in hand with marksmanship. To discuss all of the state's murders that might meet De Quincey's exacting standards would necessitate, not a volume, but an encyclopedia. And so it is contemporary interest which, more than anything else, has dictated the choices for this collection.

I have deliberately omitted several recent cases that excited great public interest and illustrated vividly the night side of human nature. Public inquiry into breaches of the law is, of course, the duty of the police, the courts, and the juries of the state, and the reporting of crimes is a legitimate concern of newspapers. But the historian may be excused if he refrains from noticing crimes of such recent date that their recounting may needlessly wound the feelings of living persons who may have been innocently involved.

The earliest date, then, among crimes presently reported is 1808, and the most recent is 1914. Of all the victims—they include, among others, a Confederate general, a lovely orphan girl, a pathetic little boy, and a highly offensive political boss—perhaps two, and no more, might have survived to this time of writing had their slayers been less pressing with their attentions. Dead, too, are most of the criminals, accusers, witnesses, man-hunters, and others directly concerned. Nobody is apt to suffer agonies of the spirit if reminded of this felony or that.

Four of the murders were committed in North Carolina's

piedmont, three in the coastal regions, and three in the mountains, which, be it suggested, sums up to something like geographical impartiality.

As to motivations, it is gratifying to establish that only two men were killed for the sordid purpose of gain. Four were crimes of vengeance, and three were what F. Tennyson Jesse describes as murders of elimination. The tenth murder was for reasons of jealousy, and those reasons were, as the evidence will show, not particularly well founded.

Of those who committed the murders, three were women; and, at risk of seeming to adopt an outworn journalistic convention, it must be recorded that two of these, also two unfortunate feminine victims, possessed exceptional beauty of person. The writer of these essays and his grave advisers are well aware that any woman involved in a major crime, whether actively or passively, is apt to be described as breathlessly lovely. Yet they, and the readers too, must accept the contemporary descriptions of these ladies, which are specific and circumstantial enough. By way of balance, the third murderess was ugly to a surpassing degree, though she was devotedly admired and courted in spite of that, and was publicly compared to the great exemplar of her avocation, Lady Macbeth.

Justice seems to have been plain but moderate in the times when these various tragedies befell and their authors were sought out for punishment. Only three of the ten killers suffered the death penalty, all of them by hanging, all of them in the mountains, and all of them manifestly and inexcusably guilty. Two others escaped the consequences of their deeds by committing suicide. There were three acquittals. One defendant so exonerated was later lynched, and to what extent he deserved lynching the reader may judge for himself. In one case the death sentence was commuted to life imprisonment, with later release on parole. One murder, and that perhaps the most cunningly and daringly devised in North Carolina's whole catalogue of violence, was never solved by officers of the law.

Only nine cases, then, came to trial, and the courts dealt with them ably and justly under the state statutes. Of the nine defendants, seven successfully sought change of venue. Six verdicts of guilty were appealed to the State Supreme Court, and for what degree of fairness and intelligence the justices disposed of those appeals the published court records may be consulted.

Since the various cases approximate separate narratives, no effort has been made to offer them in any deliberate order, chronological or otherwise, except where two murders in the mountains showed certain curious similarities that made convenient their inclusion together in a sort of double-barrelled essay.

The facts have not been embroidered with romantic conjecture. Direct quotation, for example, is always from some contemporary account, with, in several instances, indirect quotation made direct by substitution of first person for third. Nor has there been need for embroidery.

For in every instance, the records of the crime and its investigation and trial go far to show us how North Carolinians lived at a certain time and in a certain place. The most obscure person, as slain or slayer, comes to the fixed attention of his fellows, and injuries and trials are singularly vivid in their expositions. The study of a well-documented murder case may tell us as much, perhaps, about those concerned as do the reports of a political campaign or of a marching, fighting army.

In short, these people died, but before they died they lived, and here is an honest effort to prove it.

Manly Wade Wellman

Chapel Hill, North Carolina
May 1, 1954

CONTENTS

DEAD AND GONE

1

The General Dies at Dusk

THE HOT SATURDAY SUN went down over Old Washington, August 14, 1880. General Bryan Grimes was going home to Grimesland in Pitt County, to his broad white house with its pillared porch and its lofty chimneys and its door that locked with a seven-inch key. Surely that evening he did not think much about his old acquaintance, violent death.

In 1861, when he was a grave-mannered plantation baron of thirty-two, Bryan Grimes had been a member of the convention that voted North Carolina out of the Union and into the Confederacy. Thereafter, Bryan Grimes had joined the Southern army as an infantry major. His regiment had been shot to pieces behind him at Seven Pines—450 killed and wounded out of 520. Promoted colonel of the survivors, he recruited them to 327, of whom 250 fell at Chancellorsville. More blood and bullets at Gettysburg, more still in the Wilderness; a brigadier, he survived Sheridan's cannonades in the Shenandoah Valley and, a major general, led the last charge of ragged gray infantry on the morning of Appomattox. Then, because he must, he gloweringly accepted the facts and terms of Lee's surrender, the furling of the Stars and Bars, the oblivion of the Confederate States of America.

A thousand had fallen at his side, and ten thousand at his right hand, but it had not come nigh him. Importunate death had seemed always to shrink back from Bryan Grimes' bearded battle-scowl. A musket ball in the foot, a rib-cracking kick from a horse—those were the only war injuries he suffered.

Fifteen years of peace had calmed but not greatly mellowed the man who, says Douglas Southall Freeman, was lacking in no soldierly characteristic. Avoiding Reconstruction's bitter squabbles, he had labored to improve his five thousand fruitful acres at Grimesland, had shown warm affection to Charlotte Grimes and their eight sons and daughters, and had been bleakly polite to most other fellow-creatures. Josephus Daniels remembered that Grimes was "fair-minded without suavity" toward tenants and poor neighbors—forty-acre farmers like Jesse Parker and Oscar Griffin and Sam Dixon, colored patch-dwellers like young Dick Chapman. A very few close acquaintances knew the warm, brave heart cloaked by that formidable reserve. Joseph John Laughinghouse, for instance, loved his neighbor Bryan Grimes as he would love an older brother. Children, too, flocked after the general and won from him the smiles he rarely lavished on adult strangers. Everyone, seemingly, wished him well.

Grimes had spent that August 14 at the pretty courthouse town of Washington in Beaufort County—Old Washington, they called it then and call it now, reminding you that it bore the great name before even the nation's capital. Stalwart, bewhiskered, wearing a linen duster and a broad hat like a preacher's, the general stowed purchases in the rear of his two-horse buggy, ordered other goods to be delivered at Grimesland during the next week. Between whiles he heard, without

entering, sidewalk arguments to the effect that Winfield
Scott Hancock would be elected president next November
or there wasn't a just and Democratic God in heaven. And he
agreed to do a favor for his old friend Tom Satterthwaite—
surely Mr. Tom's twelve-year-old son Bryan could ride with
Grimes to the home of an uncle, Colonel J. B. Stickney, just
this side of Grimesland Plantation. Let the boy hop in. He'd
be at his uncle's in time for supper.

Grimes let his young passenger drive the buggy away on
one last errand, a happy responsibility for a twelve-year-old
who loved good horses. The general himself waited in front
of the store of S. R. Fowle & Son, speaking gravely with John
W. Smallwood of Smallwood Plantation. The buggy rolled
up. "Excuse me, I must be getting home," said Grimes, and
got in and took the reins.

They rolled out of town across the bridge that spanned the
broad Pamlico River, to Pitt County beyond. Bryan Grimes
himself had once owned that bridge and operated it for toll,
then had sold it to the state. Little Bryan prattled worship-
fully, the old soldier rejoined with quiet, understanding cour-
tesy. Leaving the main Pitt County Road, they followed a
tree-bordered wagon lane to Bear Creek. The sun was drop-
ping behind the leafy tops of oaks, cypresses, and sweet gums.
All was quiet save for the roll of wheels, the plodding fall of
hoofs. If you'd asked most folks right then, they'd have
guessed that General Grimes, healthy and vigorous at fifty-
one, had a good quarter-century of life ahead of him.

The woods crowded the banks of Bear Creek. In their
depths, a hunter could stalk and shoot deer and sometimes a
bear, if he did not disdain to wade in swampy pools. That dry
August, only a slow trickle marked the Bear Creek ford.
Grimes pulled up his horses to let them drink before finishing

the last three homeward miles. As they dipped their grateful noses, he leaned back in his seat beside the boy. A dozen yards from his left elbow grew two big, gnarly-kneed cypresses.

From between those trunks crashed out a shattering explosion. A puff of smoke rose like a gray ghost in the early evening, and there was a momentary hail-like rattle among the hoops of the carriage top.

Frightened, the horses sprang forward, splashed across the creek and bustled the swaying buggy up the far bank. Almost instinctively the general dragged powerfully on the reins, bringing the team to a halt, then swung around to stare back.

Bryan Satterthwaite, peering in terror, saw, or fancied that he saw, a figure backing away into the swampy brush.

"What are you doing there?" shouted Grimes.

The dark cypresses gave him silence. Then the general sagged forward from the waist.

"Bryan," he mumbled in his beard, "I am shot."

"Are you much hurt, General?" tremulously demanded the lad.

"Yes." The word was barely audible. "It will kill me."

Grimes' broad felt hat dropped from his head. He sank upon his buckling knees. Then his booted feet slid out of the carriage to the left, and he sprawled prone in the bottom.

Young Satterthwaite acted with pluck and presence of mind beyond his twelve years. His small hands snatched up the reins that had fallen from the general's big ones. Slapping the free ends on the rumps of the horses, he called out to them. They began to trot away from Bear Creek and the cypresses and the gun that had roared between them. Driving swiftly and capably, with the silent body at his young feet and the night thickening upon him, the boy brought carriage and team to the door of a man named Carow. There he pulled up and called shrilly for help.

Carow ran out, and stood staring and dithering. He was one of those who, in emergencies, can never say or do anything helpful. The pre-adolescent at the reins was more reliable in the crisis.

"Help me get his legs into the carriage," he begged, and this much the unstrung Carow made himself able to do. Then, still wisely, little Bryan Satterthwaite decided to tarry no longer with so sorry a companion. He whipped up and drove another mile, to the home of his uncle.

Colonel Stickney hurried out into the gloom to hold a lantern over Grimes. Blood soaked the left sleeve of the general's duster as he lay without motion. Stickney recognized, from a full and stern war experience, the condition of death. Lifting the lantern, he stared at the pock-marks of big buckshot on the hoops of the carriage top. Then he leaped in beside his nephew and drove Bryan Grimes home.

Summoned to the broad porch of Grimesland manor house, Charlotte Grimes heard what Colonel Stickney and Bryan Satterthwaite had to say about the silent form out there in the carriage. She was gentle, loving, and brave. Mastering her grief before the man and the boy, she said softly, "Don't tell the children just now."

News travelled fast. Through the small hours of the night gathered neighbors, to offer what help and comfort they could. A doctor examined the body, and found that a single buckshot had pierced Grimes' left biceps and had ploughed into his body to the heart. On the next day, a crowd of mourners saw Bryan Grimes buried with his kinsmen in the family graveyard under the live oaks. A second gathering, armed with rifles and pistols and stern in the desire to furnish Pitt County with another homicide, prowled the banks of Bear Creek on either side of the ford.

The leader of this group was Joseph John Laughinghouse, who could, on proper occasion, be far grimmer than his name. This neighbor and friend of Bryan Grimes had served as a Confederate infantry captain at the unlikely age of sixteen. In 1868, before he attained his majority, he badly beat a Reconstructionist sheriff, and when haled to court roundly cursed Judge Edmund W. Jones, nicknamed Jaybird. For this he drew a thirty-five-day sentence for contempt of court and was royally fed every day of the thirty-five by admiring ladies of his acquaintance. These experiences and characteristics made him an ideal choice to head the Pitt County Ku Klux Klan in 1870. Now, on the banks of Bear Creek, he spoke like the commander of a combat force. He had notions about who had fired that shotgun and crashed his way into the rank summer growth beyond the cypresses.

Half dammed by brush and thick, snake-sheltering grass, the stream overflowed into a swampy expanse. Those who adventured after Laughinghouse found a pathway ready chopped for them. Somebody had prepared a line of retreat for his own use. Here, pointed out Laughinghouse, was proof of premeditation, and more. The killer must have known that Grimes would drive that way on Saturday evening. He must be a neighbor as well as a deadly enemy. Who? Laughinghouse offered an answer.

Howell Paramore was a tall, slender man of some thirty years, who with his brother W. B. (just that; he was familiarly known only by the initials) operated a big country store at Nelson's Crossroads near Grimesland. Acquaintances reckoned Howell Paramore something of a dandy. He wore fine clothes. A blond moustache and imperial lent elegance to his pink face. He spoke deeply and softly. His courtly manners reminded some of a senator, others of a riverboat gambler. And, Laughinghouse remembered, Howell Paramore had quarrelled bitterly with Grimes over where a property line ran between parcels of their land. Later, a mill house at Grimesland had caught fire, and stock had died after drinking water from a plantation well. Grimes had thought that well was poisoned, had been gathering evidence on which to accuse and prosecute Howell Paramore. And now Grimes was dead of a cowardly ambuscade.

While Laughinghouse said all these things, he waded with his friends along the axe-cleared lane. Most of it was under ankle-deep water; but, where a muddy hummock rose into view, appeared a plain, fresh footprint.

They stopped and looked. It was the track of a very small shoe—size six, estimated one man. That would be a sort of exoneration for Howell Paramore. Though slender, he was tall and well-knit, and so was his brother W. B. Both of them had feet big enough to support considerable bony structure.

They might have been left alone, those Paramore brothers, but they fled that Sunday from their store at Nelson's Crossroads. Perhaps, argued some, they feared being hanged to the nearest gum or cypress, without the tiresome formality and expense of a trial. Nobody went looking for them. Laughinghouse and the others were asking about some Grimesland neighbor who owned a dainty foot and a shotgun.

Said the columns of the Raleigh *Farmer and Mechanic*, six days after the murder: "The whole county's alive with men determined to ferret out the perpetrator of this damnable and cold-blooded deed." But several days more were to pass before there was any real agreement as to who the perpetrator might be.

Young William Parker, twenty-three-year-old son of the thrifty farmer Jesse Parker whose forty acres lay near Grimesland, stood five feet six inches tall. He carried rather more lazy flesh than his small bones needed, and possessed hands and feet almost aristocratically tiny. Lacking his father's industry, he performed occasional odd jobs to get spending money. Habitually he had loafed, chewed tobacco, and drunk whiskey at the store lately operated by the now fugitive brothers Paramore. Those intent on avenging Bryan Grimes combed their memories for what William Parker might have said and done recently.

True enough, neither word nor behavior suggested any bad feeling between Grimes and the Parkers. Yet Oscar Griffin said that, in midafternoon of August 14, he had seen young Parker near Bear Creek. Griffin could not remember a shotgun, but Ed Dixon knew that Parker owned such a weapon and was skilful with it. And so M. J. Fowler, a mild-mannered ex-policeman of Old Washington, took to walking the dim trails through the Pitt County woods and to questioning those he met.

On Sunday, September 19, he talked to twenty-year-old Dick Chapman, a colored turpentine-dipper. What Chapman told him was matter for serious argument in days to follow, but that evening Fowler brought Chapman to Old Washington and asked Sheriff G. W. Dixon to lock him up as a material witness. Next morning, Fowler returned to the Grimesland neighborhood and arrested William Parker on a charge of murder.

If we may credit an opinion published in the Granville County *Express*, William Parker was "completely without money or credit, worth or character." More colloquially and pungently, his respectable acquaintances would call him ornery, sorry, and trifling. But he possessed a loyal and helpful father. Not many hours after William's arrest, Jesse Parker retained lawyers. Most notable of these was James Evans Shepherd, already brilliant and influential at thirty-three. To pay the fees, Jesse Parker readily mortgaged his little farm.

A preliminary hearing was scheduled for September 25 before Justice William P. Campbell, and upon Chapman's evidence much would depend. Fowler made a written statement of his conversation with the young Negro, and it exists in printed form today. Chapman, said Fowler, had seen Parker in the woods on the afternoon of the murder, and Parker had fired a load of squirrel shot from his gun and rammed down a charge of buckshot; then, saying he would lie in wait for General Grimes at Bear Creek, Parker left Chapman at about three o'clock. "The next day," Fowler quoted young Chapman, "I heard at Evonstein's store that Gen. Grimes was killed, and I knew from what Parker had told me that it was Parker that had killed him. The evening of the same day I saw Parker and he told me that he had killed General Grimes and that he was afraid he would be suspicioned. If he was, he wanted me to swear that we were in the woods together on the day of the murder until sunset, and that we went to Sam Dixon's house and stayed all night."

But, before Justice Campbell, Chapman would say nothing of the kind. He was maddeningly vague about his meeting with Parker on August 14. When Solicitor George Sparrow prompted him sharply, Chapman said he had been told to "be careful in talking to anyone."

"Who said that?" demanded Sparrow.

"That man there advised me to do it," said the Negro, pointing at Attorney Shepherd.

At once Shepherd said that he had given such advice only

to Parker, who had been sitting in a cell next to Chapman's. And Parker, went on Shepherd, had been threatened in jail— a detective had pointed a pistol at him, ordering him to confess. There was almost a commotion in the Justice's office, and then the solicitor himself said that there was no suggestion that Shepherd had acted improperly. Still Chapman would give no clear evidence, and he was released.

When the case went to trial on December 13, before Judge D. Schenck in the ancient massive courthouse at Old Washington, Chapman's name was not included among the witnesses for the state.

Three special prosecutors helped George Sparrow—Judge D. C. Fowle, L. C. Latham, and G. H. Browne, Jr. All were old friends of the murdered Grimes, and all were coldly determined to convict the man charged with killing him. The clerk read out the indictment, and, at the judge's gesture, William Parker rose from the prisoner's bench.

A close-wedged crowd of spectators turned its multiple gaze upon him. Parker wore neat, new clothes, complete with coat, white shirt, and necktie, as though to do honor to the occasion. A reporter noted that Parker was of fair complexion with a heavy brown moustache and was not bad-looking. He faced Judge Schenck with a show of bold assurance.

"How say you to this charge?" asked the clerk. "Are you guilty or not guilty?"

"Not guilty, sir," Parker almost boomed and sat down again. He cocked a booted foot, size six, on the bench and chewed tobacco with slow relish. The prosecution opened by calling young Bryan Satterthwaite to the stand.

Little Bryan's story of General Grimes' last drive was interrupted by frequent objections from Parker's three attorneys, and later the boy was soundly and exhaustively cross-examined.

Oscar Griffin followed, to say that he had met Parker near Bear Creek at midafternoon of August 14, and his testimony was corroborated by John Blount. These and other state's witnesses endured the shrewdly blistering attentions of Shepherd and his colleagues. The stories of the witnesses were interrupted again and again, for arguments over points of law, relevance of testimony, propriety of questions. Four whole days passed while the state conducted its hampered parade of evidence. On December 18, Judge Fowle announced that the prosecution rested. Attorney Shepherd moved for dismissal on grounds of insufficient evidence and, when the court overruled his motion, opened for the defense.

But he had not spoken more than half a dozen prefatory words when interruption came from the jury box. Juror Asa Pinkham announced shakily that he was sick, and assuredly he looked it. He trembled, writhed, and grimaced with pain. Judge Schenck declared a recess and set a bailiff scurrying to bring a doctor.

That doctor diagnosed Pinkham's ailment as "extreme nervous prostration." There was talk of bringing a cot for him to lie on while the trial proceeded, but Pinkham protested that the courtroom and all who spoke and moved within it had taken on a dreamy blur to his awareness. The doctor said flatly that Pinkham could not properly discharge his duties as a juror. Judge Schenck was forced to declare a mistrial, and ordered William Parker back to jail.

Citizens speculated at length, over Christmas dinner tables, on what evidence the defense lawyers would have offered on Parker's behalf. Those lawyers themselves concentrated on a plea for change of venue, arguing that both Beaufort and

Pitt counties were too full of the dead man's friends to guarantee fairness or even safety to Parker. The change was granted, and the new trial set for the June term of court in Martin County.

This county, to the north of Beaufort, had a reckonable proportion of citizens who had deplored secession and the Confederacy and all who had upheld such things in 1861. The war record of Byran Grimes counted against his memory with old Unionists, some of whom were apt to say that he was better off dead.

Some degree of sympathy for the accused filtered through the whole state. The *Farmer and Mechanic* inquired editorially if the right man were standing trial. Pauper the defendant surely was, but was he a murderer as well? Echoing these questions, Pitt County residents wondered what had become of the vanished Howell Paramore.

Their wonder was allayed toward the latter part of May, 1881, by news from the magnolia-swaddled town of Cheraw in South Carolina. To Cheraw had come, about noon of May 13, a stranger tall and slim, blond of moustache and chin-tuft, low-voiced, thirtyish, with manners good enough to please even South Carolinians. He had engaged a room in a hotel, and in the quiet evening had lain down on the bed and fired a pistol bullet into his temple. A day or so later, someone looked long and carefully at the corpse and said that it was Howell Paramore. His brother W. B. made no such clear return to public notice, but a later story says that he ventured deep into the South, and there was imprisoned for well poisoning. The ghosts of the dead Grimesland stock must have pricked up their shadowy ears when the tale was told.

On June 16, the charges against Parker were read out

again, before Judge John A. Gilmer, at Williamston in Martin County.

The courtroom was packed with a larger, denser throng than before, and there were two extra lawyers. Harry W. Stubbs had joined the battery of prosecutors, while the defense counsel, too, counted a fourth colleague—James A. Moore, who wielded a considerable influence in his native Martin County and who deserved his reputation for adroit court-room strategy.

Again the state called its witnesses. No court stenographer kept a formal transcript of the testimony, but the unofficial reports are to the effect that Attorney Shepherd and his associates cross-examined even more sharply and at greater length than before. They were well aware of the terms in which men would attempt to swear away William Parker's life, and skilfully they had prepared themselves.

Bryan Satterthwaite, by this time thirteen years old, was again the star witness for the prosecution. He lived on into his twenties, clerking in Fowle's store at Old Washington and dying of tuberculosis while still young; but, had he lived to the present day, he would still remember, wincingly, his two hours on the stand at Williamston.

For perhaps the prosecutors were overzealous, perhaps the boy himself was overimaginative. In any case, he testified that he had seen General Grimes' murderer plain under those cypress trees by Bear Creek, and that it was William Parker. Upon this declaration the defense attorneys pounced like minks upon a setting hen.

Not one cross-examiner, but four, took turns in haranguing and confusing the increasingly wretched, stammering youngster. Had not young Bryan sat at the right of General Grimes as the horses paused to drink? Yes, and had not the shotgun fired from the left, and wasn't the general's substantial, duster-clad body in the way, and wasn't the body hard to see through? On top of that, wasn't this story different from the one Bryan had told under oath six months before? When it came to that, wasn't he shaky about the nature of an oath—the truth, the whole truth and nothing but the truth? Did he really want to swear a man's life away like this, particularly if Judge Fowle and those other lawyers had rehearsed him in what to say, and. . . .

Six days of state witnesses, most of them subjected to fierce inquisition, but none suffering as had the unhappy youngster beside whom General Grimes had fallen. When at last the state rested its case, Attorney Shepherd rose. With something of triumph in his rich voice, he announced that the defense saw no reason or necessity to introduce any evidence whatsoever.

On the next day, June 22, the prosecution lawyers addressed the jury, fiercely demanding that William Parker be found guilty of a brutal and cowardly murder and punished for it by a stretching of his plump neck. Then came the gentlemen of the defense, with four pleas equally stirring. Notable were the speeches of Shepherd and Moore, dwelling comprehensively on the testimony of the state's young star witness and upon his later wilting under cross-examination. On June 23, the jury went to its room, elected a foreman and began to deliberate.

The Tarboro *Southerner* carried a good news account of the trial and maintained less than reportorial dispassion in predicting that Parker would be found guilty. Yet, added the court-wise correspondent, "the two most uncertain things in life are the result of a town election and the verdict of a jury."

Which aphorism proved true enough that same evening. The jury had supper in its room, then returned to its box and declared William Parker not guilty.

Parker, who had sat quietly and even carelessly through his days in court, even now betrayed little emotion. More noticeably affected was Judge Gilmer. He bent upon the jury a scowl of frank displeasure, then he looked at Parker. "Never allow your conduct to be questioned again," he said in dismissal.

To which Parker wisely answered nothing, but left the courtroom a free man and did not return to his native Pitt County. This, too, was practical wisdom, for a number of his old neighbors had voiced their intention of performing upon him their notion of a sounder justice than that administered by the Martin County jury. He stayed away—in what remote place, no surviving statement informs us.

But echoes of the case did not die. The unappeased Laughinghouse felt, and said, that Attorney Shepherd had tampered with the evidence of Dan Chapman, and that he had actively stirred up public opinion on Parker's behalf before the second trial in Martin County. In October, 1882, while Shepherd was running for judge of superior court, Laughinghouse published a paid advertisement in the *Farmer and Mechanic*, setting forth his charges against Shepherd in language that, even so late in history, might be considered as a challenge to a mortal duel. Shepherd was elected notwithstanding, and let friends talk him out of paying any attention to Laughinghouse's published criticisms. Six more years passed, and another political year was upon North Carolina.

The State Democratic party called its convention in Raleigh on May 30, 1888. Several hundred delegates heard speeches, resolutions, and predictions of triumph. Judge D. C.

Fowle, who once had prosecuted Bryan Grimes' accused slayer, was nominated as governor to the accompaniment of wild rebel yells. A slate of candidates for lesser offices was presented and voted on, name by name. On the second day of the convention rose the question of a vacancy on the bench of the State Supreme Court.

How about Judge James Evans Shepherd, asked someone. He was competent, distinguished, popular. More cheers— and a sudden lion's roar as Delegate John Joseph Laughinghouse of Pitt County surged to his feet and gained attention by sheer power of lungs.

"Will the convention endorse that damned scoundrel?" he yelled, so loudly that the windows rattled.

A deafening chorus of surprised, angry protests answered him. A delegate shook a fist in his face and Laughinghouse, never one to shrink from violence, shook his own in reply. More angrily still, Laughinghouse literally shouted down the chairman who declared him out of order. He stormed up the aisle toward the rostrum.

Suddenly there spoke a quick, calm voice of reason. "Let him speak," it urged, "and then let me answer."

That was Charles B. Aycock, not yet thirty years old and almost unknown outside his native Wayne County. Twelve years later he himself would be governor. Other delegates supported his sensible suggestion, and Laughinghouse was admitted to the platform. He repeated his charges of subornation of perjury and illegal influence on public and jury, and asked that the convention renounce Shepherd.

To this, Aycock replied as he had promised, with an even dignity that was the more effective by contrast. He said that Laughinghouse spoke sincerely but had taken rumor for fact. Shepherd's record and character, added Aycock, would surely withstand such an attack. Dramatically, another candidate for the Supreme Court judgeship rose to withdraw his own name from the race lest he be thought hopeful of profiting by the charges against Shepherd. The convention voted to nominate Shepherd, and in time he rose to be Chief Justice in his state; but when he died, at sixty-four, those who knew him best said that he carried to his grave a heart sorely wounded by Laughinghouse's accusations.

The eighth anniversary of the murder of Bryan Grimes came and went. November 2 dawned, with the election only five days away. The Democrats of Pitt and Beaufort counties had no doubt of Judge Fowle's winning the governorship, but had grave doubts of Grover Cleveland's power to beat Benjamin Harrison and stay in the White House.

Some of them muttered gloomily on the streets of Little Washington that evening after supper.

It is not certain at just what hour William Parker returned to the town, but the sun had set when a group of loungers on a corner became aware of his presence. He was thirty-one years old now. In exile he had gained flesh—his youthful plumpness had increased to a gross bulge—but not wit or prudence. He had been drinking, and he wanted to talk.

Probably no one in the party liked William Parker, and some of them must have despised him. Yet he hailed them with alcoholic good humor. He showed no trace of the calm restraint that had characterized him in jail and at his two trials. When someone reminded him, with blunt directness, that a number of people thereabouts still thought that he had killed Bryan Grimes, he replied with pot-valiant laughter and cheerful admission that the belief was a correct one.

It would appear that, in seven years and more away from home, Parker had found the time utterly to forget Judge

Gilmer's excellent advice about never again allowing his conduct to be questioned. For, it has been remembered, he began to talk frankly, even smugly, about how he had killed Bryan Grimes.

Why not tell about it now? It was funny, really—what laughter his hearers kept to themselves, he supplied in raucous gusts. Superfluously he reminded the group that he had stood trial for the murder and that a jury had found him not guilty. He delighted, did William Parker, in the familiar point of law that forbids any defendant to stand twice in legal jeopardy. Now that he was safe, now that the excitement and unpleasantness had surely died down, he would take great pleasure in straightening out his old acquaintances on the subject.

More citizens ambled close to listen. He had a considerable audience by now, and apparently it inspired him. For into those fascinated ears on all sides of him, William Parker now poured a tale that anyone would stand quiet to hear.

He himself had never felt any great animosity toward General Bryan Grimes, except such as might be caused by envy of a man in comfortable circumstances, or by irritation at a reserved and lofty manner. No, the man who had hated Grimes, even to wishing and urging his assassination, had been Howell Paramore. Remember how Grimes planned to prosecute the blond-imperialled storekeeper for arson and well-poisoning? Howell Paramore had made with Parker a sound and profitable business agreement. For shooting down General Grimes, Parker had been given a suit of new clothing—it had looked good in those two courtrooms, hadn't it?—and a saddle horse, and $100 in cash. Parker had swapped the squirrel shot in his gun for buckshot, sliced himself a lane through the swamp at the Bear Creek ford, and waited for Grimes to come driving home at dusk.

It was just as simple as that. Parker wound up by repeating his observation that nobody could badger him about the case.

Meanwhile, a town policeman had joined the sizable knot of listeners. It must be regretted that no clear identification of this sensible and articulate officer can be made today. As Parker finished talking, the policeman had some opinions of his own to voice. He began by agreeing that the statutes of North Carolina protected a defendant from standing in multiple jeopardy, but he added that the town ordinances of Old Washington included definite strictures and penalties against drunkenness and disorder. Further, it was his certain belief that Parker was guilty of both of these misdemeanors in a high degree. He finished by inviting the returned prodigal to consider himself under arrest and led him away, on small feet that both strutted and staggered, to the town jail at the rear of the firehouse.

There he locked Parker in, with no formal charge, and went to report to the town officials. Apparently there was a conference that night on the question of how to bring some sort of proper punishment to William Parker, the boastful confessor of murder from ambush. If so, nothing was decided. Nor did anything need decision.

Darkness succeeded dusk. The firehouse seemed to slumber in its girdling chinaberry trees. Parker sat in his cell and spoke no word. Probably he was beginning to realize that he had excited, not the admiration, but the astonishment of his hearers out there on the street. In the corridor a gentle old Negro janitor named Rafe Long plied a broom. It was nearly midnight when old Rafe finished his chores of tidying up and set the broom in his corner. He opened the outer door and looked into a bunched array of masked faces.

Before he could move, to retreat or to slam the door again, the first of the masked men was inside, shoving him roughly back. In came the others—maybe a dozen, maybe fifteen; Rafe could not be sure. A stern voice, which Rafe later swore he did not recognize, bade him step into an empty cell. He obeyed, and the door was shut upon him, but not locked.

Rafe listened in the blackness. Heavy blows shook the jail. The door of another cell was being broken down, and Rafe could guess which cell it was.

Then commotion, a multiple scuffle, a sound of dragging feet and panting lungs. Finally a cry of shrill, unmanned terror:

"Murder!"

No question of whose voice cried out that word.

"Murder!" screamed William Parker again; and, a third time, "Murder!"

That was his last cry. Probably a hand or a gag closed his mouth. Tramping boots echoed in the corridor and died away. Rafe came out, shaking in every limb. He was alone in the jail building. Creeping to the front door, he gazed out among the chinaberries. No human figure moved.

Sagely Rafe Long congratulated himself on being safe and unhurt. He decided that all this added up to white folks' business, and that he would not profit himself or anyone else by running to make report, just then. He walked home.

At 3:00 A.M., the small river steamer *Beta* chugged slowly up the Pamlico River near Washington. Up ahead was the bridge to Pitt County, the bridge that once had been operated for toll by Bryan Grimes, the bridge across which Grimes had driven on the evening of August 14, 1880, and beyond which, later that same evening, he had died of a buckshot in his heart.

The lookout at the bow of the *Beta* spied a pendulous something and yelled out a warning. The engines backed water, the craft idled close in the current.

A pudgy body swung by a rope from the bridge timbers. Its feet, amazingly small for so broad a man, hung flaccidly within less than a yard of the Pamlico's waters. Two of the crew swiftly cut the body loose and laid it upon the deck. To the front of the rumpled coat was pinned a paper. By the steamer's running lights, they could read three words:

JUSTICE AT LAST.

William Parker's lifetime height of five feet six inches had been considerably increased by a grotesque stretching of the neck.

The news was heard with great interest and without much sorrow all through the seaboard counties. The editor of the Washington *Progress* employed only a perfunctory dilution of diplomacy, and a thinly veiled dig at Justice James Shepherd, in his published observation.

"We very much regret this circumstance," he wrote, "and that the fair name of our town has been stained by such a lawless act; but one hears on every side the expression—that this is but the beginning of the end, and that the day is fast approaching when shrewd lawyers and packed juries will be powerless to prevent the punishment of crime in Eastern North Carolina."

Perfunctory, too, was the investigation by police and sheriff's officers. Nobody noticed any great stir toward identification of those masked men who took William Parker out of his cell and hanged him to the bridge that once had belonged to his victim.

Might Joseph John Laughinghouse have hurried over from Pitt County to lead the lynching party? It was possible, though his was a nature that would more likely dictate single and open combat rather than masked murder. Might Bryan Satterthwaite, now twenty years old, have borne a hand? It could be, it could be. But it wasn't sensible or neighborly to make vain guesses about Laughinghouse or Satterthwaite, or anybody else.

Now that it was all over, a majority of the citizens agreed that there never had been much mystery, at that, about who had killed General Bryan Grimes. The real mystery was about who had killed Parker.

As far as folks were concerned, it could stay a mystery. And so it has stayed.

2

Arsenic and Old Fayetteville

"BEAUTY ITSELF," wrote William Shakespeare, "doth of itself persuade the eyes of men without an orator."

But there was oratory to match, almost but not quite, the matchless beauty of the young widow on trial for her life in Fayetteville late in 1850; and, since in those days juries were necessarily made up of adult males, the verdict need surprise no reader of this narrative.

Fayetteville was then a town of more than 4,600 souls, free and slave, the largest in population, except for New Bern, in the whole state. It was the busy anchorhead of the Cape Fear River, the center of a rich farm region, with a number of factories and warehouses. A handsome new business district had replaced the one burnt to ashes in the disastrous fires of 1831 and 1845. The town was progressive and pleasant and prosperous, and to it came numerous northerners in the 1840's, eager to improve their fortunes by trade or business. One of these was young Alexander C. Simpson, from Esperance in upstate New York.

Alexander Simpson found the citizens of Fayetteville instantly hospitable and friendly. He opened a shop for the making and selling of carriages, hired workmen, and flourished. "Troops of friends cheered him on," an acquaintance was flamboyantly to remember. "None knew him but to love him. Perhaps the sun never shone on a kindlier youth."

Though industrious and respectable, young Mr. Simpson was not healthy, or thought himself not healthy, which sometimes comes to the same thing. He complained frequently of chills and of his digestion, and suffered from a chronic rash on face and body, possibly an allergy. For these disorders he was much under the care of doctors. He kept bottles of medicine at home and also at his carriage shop, wherewith regularly to dose himself. Such conversation and behavior suggest the hypochondriac, and perhaps the carriage maker was not quite so warmly and universally loved as the tribute just quoted might indicate.

But he was able, for all his professed infirmities, to admire a supremely lovely girl, Ann Carver. Many admired her, then and thereafter. Of surviving descriptions, the most comprehensive is also the most ungallant, for it was furnished by officers of the law: ". . . a woman of small stature, has very black hair, dark complexion, large black eyes, small nose and large mouth, with her upper lip straightly projecting." These features, taken in combination, can be very prepossessing, as in Ann Carver's case they were. Probably there was something Latin in her aspect, and her figure did high justice to the mid-century fashions of snug bodice and abundant skirt, flounced or crinolined. She was not wealthy—her mother was a widow who kept a boarding house—and she decided, or was persuaded, to turn from a childhood sweetheart to Alexander Simpson, with his chills, his rash, and his carriage-making business. They were married in 1846, when she was sixteen and he somewhere in his early thirties.

About the names of Ann and Alexander Simpson still hovers the garlicky odor ascribed by learned men to arsenic under analysis; echoes the strident clash of attorneys' cry and counter-cry; whispers the more stealthy voice of an ill-favored old enchantress, pronouncing incantation and prophecy; crouches the cloaked figure of tragedy without official solution. A whole fabric of legend has spun itself during the century since.

Alexander brought his bride to a comfortable two-story house on Gillespie Street, not far from the Market House that stands today. From acquaintances he hired three Negro slaves to wait upon her. In the Simpson home lodged and boarded two exemplary and mannerly young workmen from the carriage shop, Samuel G. Smith and A. H. Whitfield. To these people the girl-wife made herself agreeable with the effortlessness of a smiling beauty, and also to neighbors and tradespeople. A notable exception seems to have been Miss Rachel Arey, a girl her own age, oldest daughter of Jacob Arey who lived across the street. Possibly, just possibly, Miss Rachel preferred that young Mr. Whitfield had a less charming landlady; in any case, the two "had a few words" and were only formally polite thereafter.

Two children were born to the Simpsons within the first two years of their marriage, and both died in infancy. No surviving comment suggests that young Mrs. Simpson greatly mourned these bereavements, but they must have contributed to her husband's great indulgence of her. With no children, and servants to do the cooking and other housework, Ann found herself with time to while away. Wherefore she strolled abroad almost daily—one conceives that she wore a chip bonnet and carried a parasol, and was the joy of all masculine beholders—and somewhere, probably early in 1849, she took to visiting a slovenly district called Benbow's Factory Row.

The attraction there was Polly Rising, a "middling old" woman who professed to be a fortune teller. Judge Robert Strange was to refer to her as "the renowned Mrs. Rising," which may have been irony; but she enjoyed some reputation in her calling, and so much did Ann Simpson enjoy having her fortune told that she visited Polly Rising several times a week. The fortune repeatedly told her was, as later sworn to in court, an exciting one. But it was not reckonably more exciting than the life Ann Simpson actually lived between visits to Benbow's Factory Row in early October of 1849.

That month, a seamstress by the name of Miss Nancy Register came daily to the house to make clothes for Ann Simpson. The carriage-maker's wife, three years married but only nineteen, liked to prattle to this woman. They grew to consider themselves good friends, as witness what followed one morning when Mr. Simpson bleakly departed, leaving on the breakfast table a note for his wife.

Ann read it and sought the room where Nancy Register was sewing. She locked the door, sat down, and read the communication aloud:

"Ann, I once thought you loved me, but now I have reasons to suspect, that you love another better than me. For the sake of your friends, you may stay in my house, but you must find your own clothes as well as you can. Prepare a bed for me up-stairs tomorrow. You can no longer be my wife."

Miss Register heard this with great interest and attention, for she was able to quote the letter under oath when more than a year had passed. Her pretty employer seemed nonplussed, as well she might in the face of this accusation and ultimatum.

"I do not know whether to let him know that I received the note," she said, "or prepare him a bed." Then, plucking up courage: "He need not turn a fool now, as James has been visiting the house ever since we were married."

The dressmaker must have known who "James" was, may even have seen him calling at the house. She gave sober council, perhaps wondering who would pay Mrs. Simpson's dressmaking bills.

"You had better act differently to what you have done," she advised sensibly, "as Mr. Simpson might kill the man that is visiting you."

"He knows better than to do it," vowed Ann at once, having regained her confidence. She threw the note in the fire, and on the following morning she told Miss Register that she would greet her husband with a kiss on his return from work. Later in the day, Miss Register saw her cuddling close to Alexander, as though they were reconciled. On the morrow, however, Ann was packing to leave. Her husband, she told Miss Register, had been "put out with her from reports." But she regarded this unpleasant situation as but temporary.

"A fortune teller told me," she elaborated, "that Mr. Simpson and I would not live together but five years, and three of them are gone, and I believe it now."

She then wrote several notes, which would make interesting reading to this day had they survived. She also said, whether at that time or in another conversation it is impossible to say: "James kisses sweeter than anyone in the whole world."

This statement, immensely complimentary to James and equally authoritative as to kissers of the world, convinced Miss Register that Alexander Simpson's accusations were not idle. But Ann elaborated. She loved James better than her husband, she announced. Indeed, once she had planned to marry him and had accepted Alexander only to get a home.

She left the house, but the separation was short. Her husband allowed her to return, though there was another quarrel. On or about October 25, she walked into Polly Rising's house, where the fortune teller's notably unsavory neighbor from next door, Ann Butler, was visiting.

Alexander Simpson, so said his lovely wife, had struck her that day with his fist—under what provocation, she did not explain. The fortune teller expressed pity and bade Mrs. Simpson not to mind it.

"Mr. Simpson will not be living this day week if you will do as I tell you to," she remarked weightily.

Which may suggest why Ann Simpson tripped gracefully into the drug store of Samuel Hinsdale on November 3 to ask the young clerk, James M. Smith, to weigh her out an ounce of arsenic.

Mr. Edmund Pearson, scholarly and philosophic regarding crime as well as regarding libraries, dime novels, and the career of Theodore Roosevelt, has deplored arsenic as a lethal weapon. In a work intriguingly called *Murder At Smutty Nose* he refers to this compound as the favorite poison of the ignorant and unimaginative. Elsewhere in the same work he speculates on the number of imaginary rats offered as excuses by arsenic buyers with murder in their hearts. Rats were mentioned by Ann Simpson to James Smith and also to a companion she called Jimmy. Was he, by the way, the admirer on whose account so much embarrassing worry had come to her? The drug clerk readily supplied the arsenic, and Ann Simpson departed.

Four days later, on Wednesday, November 7, she presided

at the noon dinner table. With her sat her husband, apparently no longer vexed with her, and the two boarders, Samuel Smith and A. H. Whitfield.

For dessert there was syllabub, a foaming dainty prepared with whipped cream and wine and spices, and perhaps also, at this particular repast, with another ingredient.

"I have made only two glasses," said Mrs. Simpson to Smith and Whitfield, "because you are Sons of Temperance."

Smith, a devout member of that abstemious organization, meditated that he had heard discussions at meetings of the Sons of Temperance much to the discredit of syllabub. Mr. Simpson, who had no such scruples, readily ate his portion with a silver spoon, and asked for more. His wife offered her own glassful, and this, too, he ate. He returned to his shop with Whitfield, Smith remaining at the house.

That evening, family and boarders gathered for coffee and conversation. Smith took a cup from his landlady's fair hand, and began to stir it with a spoon. Ann Simpson said something to him and repeated it in a sharp tone.

"Mr. Smith," she called out so sternly that he jumped, "I said that was Mr. Simpson's coffee."

Smith passed it to his employer, who drank. When he had finished, Ann took the cup from his hand, turned it this way and that, stared at the grounds in the bottom, and proposed to tell his fortune. Her manner was creepy enough to do credit to Polly Rising herself.

"I see," she declared, "a sick bed, a coffin, and a dark and muddy road with clouds around." An impressive pause. "You know, lovey, I had my fortune told once; I was to marry you, have two children, and both were to die. I was to have a third, it was to live, and then you were to die."

Such prattle did not charm Alexander, who changed the

subject to say that he felt ill. He often said as much, and nobody was alarmed. Smith, who liked Ann and admired her beauty, now asked her to tell his fortune.

She saw nothing in Smith's coffee grounds so baleful as the fate she had promised her husband. "Your fortune," she said, "is that you shall go and see a young lady shortly." This prediction Smith took "jocularly," as he later phrased it, and he departed. Probably he called on the young lady foretold him, and he may have wished that she was as lovely as Mrs. Ann Carver Simpson.

But Alexander, meanwhile, felt worse by the minute. At early bedtime he complained of an upset stomach, and he spent a restless, uncomfortable night. On Thursday morning, November 8, Ann sent her servant boy Charles to fetch Dr. William P. Mallett.

This young physician was no Sherlock Holmes, to deduce at once a stealthy poisoning; but even a John Watson could have seen that Simpson was seriously ill. He vomited and complained of a burning sensation in his stomach. Dr. Mallett made him up some pills of calomel and opium. Returning after noon, he found his patient worse and administered morphine. Ann Simpson was at her husband's bedside and put her slim hand on his brow. He turned away.

"You are a touch-me-not!" she chided him.

While Simpson thus agonized, his wife went down to take dinner with Smith and Whitfield, delighting them with her bright conversation. Turning to Smith, she asked suddenly about the effect of arsenic upon rats. He replied that there were two kinds of arsenic, red and white. If rats ate the red, he continued, they ran toward fire; if they ate the white, they ran into water. This small talk of the table broke off when the sick man moaned piteously, and Smith went upstairs with

Ann. There he watched Ann give her husband a brown pill in a spoonful of syrup, and she expressed satisfaction that Alexander did not vomit it up again.

By evening the lady opined to Smith that her husband was "unduly scared, begging the doctor like a child to come and see him." She put a hot poultice on the shipwrecky stomach, and sent Whitfield to fetch Dr. Benjamin Robinson. It may have been Whitfield who stopped at the Arey home across the street and asked Miss Rachel to come also.

Despite her earlier quarrel with Ann, this resolute and compassionate girl was a good friend of Alexander. She came to the house and into the sick room. The carriage-maker lay in a cold sweat, under the calm gaze of his wife. He turned on his bed to say to Miss Rachel that he was dying and asked her to pray for him.

Greatly moved, Rachel said that she could not pray and bade him pray for himself. Again he shifted on the bed, his face to the wall. "Lord Jesus, have mercy on me," he muttered, and those were his last recorded words. Dr. Mallett had come by now, and with Dr. Robinson watched Alexander Simpson lapse into a coma. Some time between eight and nine o'clock that night, he died.

Now Ann sought out Rachel. Evidently forgetting all coldness between them, she became confidential. She told of Polly Rising's prediction—that Alexander would live but one week and that she, Ann, would then marry her early love. Rachel stared, aghast. There was not a tear in the large dark eye of Ann Simpson.

Dr. Mallett approached the widow. He inquired if she were pregnant, and she said that she was not. Then he suggested that a post mortem examination be made.

To the doctor it seemed that Ann Simpson exhibited

neither more nor less repugnance than he might expect from any freshly bereaved wife so urged.

"Why should it be made?" she asked, and he replied, "For my own satisfaction."

"If you and Dr. Robinson desire it, and regard it as important," she then said, "I will interpose no objection."

The two doctors carried the body away. How Ann Simpson rested that first night of her widowhood has not been described. Next morning, however, Rachel Arey beheld her dressed in "a lovely pink silk dress with a lot of lace on it, and a pink bow of ribbon in her hair. . . ." By way of mourning, she wore a narrow band of black velvet around her bare throat.

That same day, Dr. Mallet and Dr. Robinson opened Alexander's body and removed the stomach. Its outside surface appeared bright red with inflammation. Probably at their direct word, Coroner Archibald Campbell called an inquest for the morning of Saturday, November 10. There the two men of medicine, with the help of several others, performed certain grisly tests. Observing these, the coroner's jury declared Alexander Simpson dead of arsenic poisoning and recommended that inquiry be made into what part his widow had played in his destruction.

Judge John Dick was then holding final sessions of the fall term of superior court in Fayetteville, and he issued a bench warrant for the arrest of Ann Simpson. Sheriff Alexander Johnson sought her at her home and elsewhere, but came back and endorsed the warrant, "not to be found." Meanwhile, on Monday, November 12, a grand jury returned a bill of indictment against the absent lady. It was couched in the language that had survived from Colonial times and before:

"The jurors for the State, upon their oath present, that Ann K. Simpson, late of the county of Cumberland, not having the fear of God before her eyes, but being moved and seduced by the instigation of the devil. . . ."

And so forward, some 2,000 words, contrastingly eloquent and cumbersomely repetitious, to the effect that Ann Simpson had dosed her husband with arsenic, first in the syllabub, then in the coffee, of which dosage Simpson "did languish, and languishing did live; on which said eighth day of November, in the year aforesaid, at and in the county of Cumberland aforesaid, of the said sickness and distemper occasioned by the drinking of the said coffee, so mixed with poison as aforesaid, died."

Small wonder, perhaps, that the Widow Simpson should flee fast and far from accusations so formidable. She was reported at Wilmington, then at Charleston, finally at Havana. A year passed. Came November 7, 1850, anniversary of those two glasses of syllabub and the coffee hour in the Simpson parlor. A new session of court convened at Fayetteville. Word came to Sheriff Johnson that he would do well to call at the La Fayette Hotel. He did so, and there he found the lovely lady he had earlier sought without avail.

She said to the sheriff that she would surrender and demand immediate trial. Her flight the year before, she explained, had been dictated by the fear that she would have to spend melancholy months in the comfortless county jail before her case was heard. The jail now received the most appetizing inmate of all its history, and five days later she was brought before Judge Dick.

In attendance upon her were sheriff's deputies, her mother, and four lawyers.

Robert Strange was chief strategist of the force. A former

judge and United States senator, he had also written a novel, *Eoneguski, or the Cherokee Chief.* Criticism in high places of its plot and style may have helped influence Judge Strange to turn from politics in 1840 and to become the recognized "pride and ornament" of the Fayetteville bar. With him were handsome, curly-haired Warren Winslow, who later served as North Carolina's governor for twenty-five days; Warren Winslow's equally prepossessing brother John; and Duncan K. McRae, an exuberant speaker even in that day of orotundity.

To help Solicitor Ashe with the prosecution, New York relatives of Alexander Simpson had hired young James Dobbin, tall, spare, and impressive, who had read his law under Judge Strange and now came to oppose him.

The bill of indictment was read aloud by Duncan C. McRae, clerk of the court and kinsman of one of the defense counsel. Making an end, he asked the prisoner how she pleaded.

"Not guilty," she replied.

"How will you be tried?" was his next question.

"By God and my country," she gave the traditional rejoinder.

"God send you a good deliverance," wound up the clerk. It must have been as good as a play.

On November 14, Thursday and proclaimed as Thanksgiving Day, the trial began before a courtroom packed to the very window sills. Ann Simpson sat in the prisoner's box, gowned and veiled becomingly in the black she had not worn earlier. Next to her sat her mother and her aunt. It was sourly commented by Judge Strange that save for these companions, women in the audience and through the town showed notable lack of sympathy for the prisoner. Of the attitude of men present nothing was said, but much may be imagined.

A jury was empanelled. It included six farmers, two merchants, two laborers, a tailor, and a turpentine-getter. Again the clerk read the redundant bill of indictment and followed it with an address to the jury on his own part.

"Upon this indictment the prisoner has been arraigned," he told them impressively, "and upon her arraignment she has pleaded not guilty, and for her trial has put herself upon God and her country; which country ye are. So that your duty is to inquire whether she be guilty of the felony and murder wherewith she stands charged, or not guilty. If you find her guilty, you shall say so; if you find her not guilty, you will say so, and no more. Sit together, hear the evidence, and give your verdict accordingly."

The evidence was immediately forthcoming, and it was of a nature that assuredly caused the six farmers, the two laborers, the two merchants, the tailor, and the turpentine-getter to sit together and hear it with fascinated interest.

The prosecution opened with testimony of the doctors concerning Alexander Simpson's death in agony and of their later research that indicated enough arsenic in his system to dispose of several men. After them followed James Smith the druggist's clerk, Nancy Register the seamstress, Rachel Arey the neighbor's daughter, Alexander Johnson the sheriff, and Ann Butler the friend of Polly Rising. Mrs. Rising herself would have ornamented the procession of witnesses most dramatically; however, as the audience must have sorrowed to hear, she had died during Mrs. Simpson's year of absence. All the 14th and 15th were taken up by this testimony for the state and by cross-examination, thorough and sometimes fierce, on the part of the defense. Upon Ann Butler, in particular, Mr. John Winslow of the defense showered questions which that unfortunate woman answered only because she must. He forced her to admit that, in the parlance of the day, she was no better than she should be—indeed, on her own confession she was considerably worse.

At 6:30 P.M. of the 15th, the state rested from what it plainly considered a towering accusation of the lovely young widow, and the defense electrified all hearers by announcing that it would present no witnesses at all.

Everyone—judge, jury, lawyers, and Ann Simpson—had a hasty supper. Then began the arguments.

That was the era of thundering courtroom eloquence, and every lawyer on both sides was an accomplished speaker. First to rise was Duncan McRae of the defense. His first forensic experience had come at the age of five, when he had recited an address of welcome to General Lafayette. Now, at thirty, he quoted, not only from works on medical jurisprudence to suggest that the tests of Dr. Mallett and Dr. Robinson were inaccurate, but also from Shakespeare, Walter Scott, and the Book of Ecclesiastes. Strongly he argued that Alexander Simpson had been unwarrantedly jealous, and that he had committed suicide by drinking poison.

When McRae had finished Mr. Solicitor Ashe rose, with medical authorities of his own, and a burning rebuttal to McRae's suggestion that Simpson had committed suicide.

"Simpson take his own life?" he demanded rhetorically. "He seek the cold embrace of death? See him as he lay on that bed of suffering! See him writhing with agony and burning up with inextinguishable heat! Hear him pleading like a child with those about him for succor! And when he is told there is no human relief for him, hear that passionate outbreak of his alarmed conscience: 'Lord Jesus Christ, have mercy on me!' It was death he feared all the while. It was death he wished to avert. It was death he struggled against to the last moment of his life. Such, gentlemen, is not the conduct of one who lays violent hands on his own life. The idea is preposterous."

The November night had fallen upon Fayetteville, but few of the spectators stirred away as this plea came to its end. The solicitor retired, and forward in turn came Warren Winslow. One fancies that he wore a tail coat with big silver buttons, a ruffled shirt and jewelled studs, and that his curly locks tossed upon his broad brow as he surpassed in emotional argument those who had preceded him. He, too, quoted Shakespeare, and Charles Dickens as well, and he elaborated speciously upon McRae's suggestion that Simpson had committed suicide. With fluent gestures he called the jury's attention to his client, who had heard the evidence with an almost graven composure, but who now sobbed with her lovely dark head upon her mother's breast.

"Gentlemen," he finished movingly, "the authorities of government appointed yesterday as a day of general thanksgiving. Our people were bidden to abstain from all secular pursuits, and to repair to their respective places of worship, there to render thanks to Almighty God for all His beneficent kindnesses. His Honor justly deemed it an act of mercy and necessity to continue the sittings of this court. Yesterday was no day of thanksgiving for my unhappy client. It was to her a day of trial, humiliation and sorrow. Today, you can make one heart glad. God grant that you may feel authorized to unloose the prison doors, and set the captive free; that today, nay, that the rest of her life may be one perpetual day of thanksgiving, to Almighty God for so great an additional mercy vouchsafed to her."

Ann Simpson continued to weep. And, as Winslow resumed his seat, he must have gloried to see that several members of the jury were shedding tears of their own.

When an attorney can produce in jurymen so manifest an evidence of sympathy for his case, he may well count himself successful. So Winslow undoubtedly felt, and it was with dismay that Mr. Dobbin rose to conclude for the prosecution.

"Eloquence, full of touching pathos and thrilling heart-stirring appeals," he said to the twelve good men and true, "have caused you, and more than you, ever and anon, to weep in sympathy for the 'poor unfortunate,' 'the poor woman' at the bar. I will neither strive to stir up your prejudices, nor bid you crush your generous sensibilities, nor murmur that you do not coldly chase away the starting tear. But I solemnly warn you as men—as sworn men—those tears are not to blot out the law!"

He cited cases of precedent, he reviewed testimony, he rehearsed the whole structure of the evidence against Ann Simpson. But he must have known, as did his opponents, that he could not marshal the reason of his hearers against their weeping. When Judge Strange took Dobbin's place, to deliver the final speech for the defense, he must have known that his side had won, as certainly as though the ghost of Polly Rising were whispering it in his ear as a forecast.

What Strange had to say about the chances that Simpson had taken his own life was careful elaboration of what McRae and Winslow had said before him. More fully he devoted himself to stimulating the pity of the jury for lovely, tearful Ann Simpson. Midnight had come, and he ventured upon a parable.

"We read that in ancient times, a citizen was once traversing the street of a populous town," he said, "when suddenly a snow-white dove flew into his bosom, and quietly nestled near the throbbing of his heart. Surprised at the incident, he cast his eyes upwards, and beheld a ravenous hawk hovering above him. He did not cast out from his bosom the timid guest, but cherished the poor bird, and saved it from the talons of its relentless foe. Gentlemen, the prisoner has, as this timid bird, come to your bosoms, escaping from those who are seeking her life, who are seeking the ruin of her fame, dearer than life. Will you, let me ask you, will you cast her forth a prey to her enemies, or, like the kind citizen, cherish and protect her?"

With this, and other arguments, he led up to his final trumpeting appeal:

"Gentlemen, into your hands we commit the prisoner—it is a precious deposit. I speak not of her fair body only, though that is much; but it bears within it a pearl of immortal price, for which God Himself poured out His blood—deal with it accordingly. There she lies before you, almost lifeless, awaiting her doom. She hath no voice to give utterance to her entreaties, not for her life only, but for her good name, dearer than life—dear not only to her, but to the many with whom she is connected. But, through us, her counsel, she is permitted to speak, and we pray you, gentlemen, to deal with her in mercy. And once more committing the prisoner to your hands, we conclude in the language of the law—'And may God send her a good deliverance.'"

Judge Dick charged the jury as to the law and the evidence. Reading his charge today, one surmises that he spoke with notable dispassion, in utter contrast to the speeches of the lawyers. At three o'clock in the morning of November 16, the jury retired to its room for deliberation. At six o'clock, in the black hour before dawn, it returned to announce its verdict.

"Not guilty."

The records do not say how Ann Simpson received this word, nor to what degree it affected the town of Fayetteville with surprise. Judge Dick ordered the widow discharged from custody, and to her was turned over the considerable estate of Alexander Simpson.

She did not remain long in Fayetteville. Again she departed for Charleston. One school of thought predicted, as had the lamented Polly Rising, that she would marry her James.

But she did not. On April 17, 1852, The *Weekly North Carolinian* carried a notice calculated to bulge the eyes of its readers:

"In Charleston, S.C. on the 4th inst. by the Reverend Mr. Gotthart Bernham, Mr. Charles Young of that city to Mrs. Ann K. Simpson of Fayetteville, N.C."

There was another wedding in town at about the same time. A. H. Whitfield, the teetotaller assistant of Alexander Simpson, married Rachel Arey. Miss Rachel lived happily ever after with her new husband and often told the tale of Alexander Simpson's death to her children. Less serenity, says legend, attended the marriage of Charles Young and Ann Simpson. A separation surely occurred, and, it was whispered, Charles Young, too, died suddenly and untimely.

And still later, another brief note in a Charleston newspaper. It is to be seen today, an undated clipping in the North Carolina Room of the library of the State University:

"SINGULAR DEVELOPMENT—*The Murderess of Two Hus-*

bands—The Milwaukie [*sic*] Sentinel says that it is believed from recent developments that Ann R. Bilansky, who was executed at St. Paul, Minnesota, for the Murder of her husband by administering arsenic, was the same person who on the 8th of November, 1849, poisoned Alex. D. Simpson, her husband, in the town of Fayetteville, N.C. In that case arsenic was the agent employed, and after the death of Simpson his wife was arrested, but succeeded in escaping to Charleston, and hence to Havana, where she remained until about May, 1850. She returned to Fayetteville on the 7th of November following, surrendering herself for trial, and was acquitted. On the trial of Mrs. Bilansky at St. Paul, she stated that she had resided at Fayetteville, N.C., where her husband died. The Christian names of the two women were identical, and many circumstances in St. Paul subsequent to her execution have been called to mind which tend to the belief that she and Mrs. Simpson were the same person."

And finally, people said and say to this day, she was brought back to Fayetteville one dark night and secretly buried at the edge of Person Street. Any romanticist would dearly love to believe all of these things.

Ann Simpson did become the heroine of a novel. In 1868, Benjamin Robinson published *Dolores: A Tale of Disappointment and Distress*. The star-crossed lady in this work is innocent of the crime of poisoning, and circumstances are blackly against her for most of the way. Critically speaking, the subtitle is most amply fulfilled—disappointing and distressing to a high degree are the stumbling prose and the grotesque characterizations. The sober and uncolored reports of the actual trial, as published by Attorney William H. Haigh, make infinitely better reading.

Whatever the fate of beautiful Ann Simpson, there is no doubt about what happened to Alexander Simpson. He died of arsenic.

Somebody gave it to him.

Who?

3

The Preacher and the Gun

THE MORNING OF Monday, November 15, 1852, broke dull, chill, and windy over the Rose Bay Community in Hyde County. Such weather, in melodramatic fiction, presages disaster. Young Clement H. Lassiter, master of what they called a "singing geography school," rose from his bed in the farmhouse of Dorset Mason. He planned to walk that day up the turnpike to spacious, magnificent Lake Mattamuskeet and never to come back.

Lassiter had arrived at Rose Bay early in the year, from his native Gatesville, to teach the school at the bend of the turnpike two miles from Mason's. His pay was $70 a quarter, by no means beggarly for the time and region. In figure he was "low-built," as North Carolinians say, about five feet six inches tall, with broad chest and shoulders. Though only in his middle twenties, he was beginning to put on flesh. He has been described as "of reserved manner and melancholy temperament," and his work as a teacher occupied almost wholly his time and thought. Yet, save for a certain exception, the people of Rose Bay liked him and made him welcome in their homes. He must have felt melancholy beyond his usual wont, to be leaving a community so friendly.

He dressed himself in a white shirt and a suit of thick black broadcloth, with a rather fancy vest of brown silk. In a new red-striped carpetbag he stowed a change of clothing. His trunk would stay at the Mason house, to be sent for later. On his head he put a rough cloth cap. Just before noon, he took leave of Dorset Mason, and his manner seemed both friendly and haunted.

Mason had boarded Lassiter since August and was sorry to see him go. Lassiter confessed to feeling uneasy about walking alone up the turnpike toward the lake.

"Anybody that would try to get his wife to swear my life away," he added, "would take my life any way he could."

But he did not name the man he feared and, if Mason knew without being told who that man was, he never said so for the records. Lassiter picked up his carpetbag and trudged off, bent on seeking employment at another school some four miles eastward on the shores of Lake Mattamuskeet.

Away from Mason's walked Lassiter, along a narrow path that joined the turnpike. Today that same road, graded and ditched, runs close to where it ran a hundred years ago. In 1852 it led from the head of Rose Bay straight for two miles eastward to the schoolhouse where Lassiter had been teaching. Thence, bending somewhat to the right, it continued another two miles or so to the lake. Along its northern side ran a deep-cut canal, connecting lake and bay. The stretch of turnpike between schoolhouse and bay was set with a dozen or so farm dwellings, which formed a settlement of sorts. From the school to the lake, however, the turnpike lay through clumps and thickets of brushy pine and laurel, with no houses whatever until it came to the shore of the lake itself.

Lassiter reached the turnpike just at the point where Thomas Bridgman lived, and Bridgman was just coming into his yard after a morning's work in the fields. With the ready hospitality of the Tarheel countryman, Bridgman invited Lassiter to his noonday dinner table. The schoolmaster accepted, for he liked good food, and very probably he did ample justice to Mrs. Bridgman's meat and vegetables. After the meal, he remained and talked until about three o'clock. Then Bridgman went into the back yard to feed his hogs, and Lassiter resumed his journey.

He must have moved at a very slow rate, for it was an hour or so later when he paused in another dooryard not quite half a mile to the eastward and shook hands with the venerable Thomas Gibbs. To reach Gibbs's home from that of Bridgman, Lassiter had been obliged to pass the fine double-chimneyed house of Rose Bay's most prosperous and remarkable citizen. While Lassiter chats briefly with old Mr. Gibbs, let us make the acquaintance of George Washington Carawan —planter, preacher, and a recognized leader of the little community.

He was born at Swanquarter in 1800 and was orphaned of his father before he was five years old. His mother was strong-minded and toiled hard to support her four children, but she is said to have been quick to anger, and she was fanatically strict in her religion. As she worked, so she required her children to work almost as soon as they could toddle.

Schools were scarce in North Carolina in the early years of the nineteenth century, and so she taught her children herself, how to read and write and do sums. "Firm but not fond," wrote a man who knew her, "her system of education was deprived of every charm, and, the task completed, no cheering word of approbation excited the child to renew application." She talked a great deal about God and still more about the terrors of hell.

Young George Washington Carawan so actively rebelled against this tuition that by the time he was fourteen the neighbors called him a wilful young sinner, profane of speech and a sarcastic foe of the staid and orthodox faith to which almost every other person of the neighborhood subscribed. He argued for the atheistic point of view, sneeringly and cleverly as well, with whomever would uphold conservative Christianity. He had a notable gift for mimicry and attended revivals held by Methodist and Baptist ministers solely for the purpose of observing their pulpit styles, then imitating them to the roaring delight of his friends.

At the age of twenty-one, he married Elizabeth Carow and moved with her to Goose Creek Island in Beaufort County. His brother Green Carawan, who had better pleased their mother by becoming a Baptist minister, served a church near by. Washington Carawan farmed for four years and toilsomely achieved some success. Then he quarreled, publicly and spectacularly, with his brother, whom he accused of trying to seduce Elizabeth. Nobody seems to have taken his angry charges seriously, and, scolding, he moved back to Hyde County. There he worked land near his mother's home, and later bought and cultivated the farm on the Rose Bay Turnpike.

He continued, both as successful farmer and as scoffer at religion, until the age of twenty-seven. Then, with characteristic abruptness, he professed conversion. At the South Mattamuskeet Baptist Church he loudly repented of his wordly mockeries and asked for baptism. He was accordingly dipped by Elder Enoch Brickhouse, amid chorused rejoicings over so incandescent a brand snatched from the burning. The baptizing elder remarked that he hoped to see his new convert become a preacher.

That would sound like a direct invitation to join the ministry; but Carawan chose to recognize a summons from a considerably higher ecclesiastic authority than Elder Brickhouse. He announced, some days after his baptism, that Jesus Christ had appeared to him in a vision, haloed in glory and had extended to him a scroll that bore a command to preach the gospel.

His fellows, simple partakers in the Old School Baptist conviction, heard this story and accepted it as unvarnished truth. He received ordination at the hands of Elders Samuel Ross and John Richardson and from the first was a shining success in the pulpit. Energetically he labored to found new churches on Cedar and Hog Islands in Cartaret County and, upon the death of his brother Green on Goose Creek Island, assumed the charge of the church there also. These and others he visited in turn, circuit-rider fashion, and never lacked for devout hearers.

His style of preaching was original and forceful. A big man of the most handsome and commanding appearance, he dominated from his pulpit. One contemporary wrote of him: "There was a strong old Saxon in his language which was captivating." Another, less educated but salty of speech for all that, vowed: "I would sit all day upon a sharp rail and listen to Carawan's preaching." He surpassed many of the most fervent exhorters, and was known far and wide for the moving prayers he addressed extempore to the Almighty. He liked to argue and debate the tenets of his denomination, and sometimes spoke in bitter criticism of other sects.

The conversions he achieved were numerous, and he himself baptized, throughout a period of nearly twenty-five years, more than five hundred men and women. Several young men so brought into the church by his efforts became preachers through his inspiration. With more education and opportunity, Carawan might have become another Henry Ward Beecher or Brigham Young among the spiritual leaders of his day.

For all this godly service, he refused any salary or other payment. His large Rose Bay farm and another broad acreage on the lake were worked by slaves, and he was comfortably well off, was even called a rich man. His first wife died in 1839, and within three weeks he had married a second time— Mary Bell, who had been his housekeeper. It is said that the suit he bought for the funeral of Elizabeth sufficed him at his wedding to Mary.

But this story, if true, is the only one which would seem to indicate stinginess in his nature. The Reverend Mr. Carawan was never over-slow at turning loose a dollar. He bought himself fine guns and liked to roam the Rose Bay Woods, shooting blackbirds. Something boyish remained in his nature, for he kept two tame bears in a stout cage in his yard. They must have delighted his three young sons, the only survivors of twenty children by his two wives. He was also rearing the orphaned son of his niece, a nineteen-year-old named Carawan Sawyer. This youth could neither read nor write, but he could, and did, drink frequently. However, he had come to bear a responsible hand in running the Rose Bay farm.

Carawan was hospitable. It is said that he made welcome all travelling strangers, with food and entertainment, and the praise of this trait in him suggests that he outdid even his neighbors in what has always been a North Carolina virtue.

At fifty-two, he was still an imposing figure of a man, more than six feet tall and of broad, muscular build. His clean-

shaven face still kept something of the good-humored hand-
someness of his youth, and he had a big nose, a firm chin, and
wide-set, brilliant eyes. His white hair, thinning above his
spacious forehead and worn long behind, gave him a venerable
aspect.

Most of the Rose Bay people deferred to him as the most
virtuous and admirable of men, and counted themselves lucky
to enjoy his company and example. However, old Mr. Gibbs
disliked him, and so also did Albin B. Swindell, a Baptist
minister like Carawan and a man both pious and courageous.
Swindell had denounced Carawan in open meeting of the
church membership, charging him with unpreacherly interest
in women and hinting of murder in Carawan's past. But
Carawan's influence and reputation enabled him to draw
from the assembly a vote of confidence and a denouncement
of Swindell as a jealous troublemaker.

And while we have tarried thus long to observe Carawan,
we have lost sight of Lassiter. It is too bad, really. After he
left the Gibbs home, only one man ever saw him alive again.

By midday of Wednesday, November 17, with rain falling
cold upon Rose Bay, Lassiter's old neighbors were wondering
about him. Word was sent to the farmers on the border of
Lake Mattamuskeet, and on Friday, Lassiter's friend, Levi
McGowan, inquired for him from door to door of that region.

Nobody had seen him arrive at the lake community. On
Saturday, November 20, farmers from both the lake and the
bay gathered and began to comb the thick woods on either
side of the turnpike, at first to no avail. The morning passed
with no clue of the vanished schoolmaster to be found.

Among those who searched were Jesse Bridgman and Jesse
Mason, relatives of the men who had heard Lassiter's fare-
wells. After noon dinner they poked here and there in a

stretch behind Jesse Bridgman's property, where fire had destroyed the timber five years before. A tangle of catclaw briers, gallbushes, reeds, and pine saplings had sprung up, and through these the two men stubbornly forced their way at midafternoon. Underfoot the ground was soggy and grown up in thick moss, like sod—a "dismal," such country was called. Scattered over this moss at one place lay some sticky clods. Jesse Bridgman noticed brown dryness among the green fronds. He knelt and scooped with both hands. His fingers closed on cloth. He tugged—it was the lapel of a coat. He had found Clement Lassiter.

Mason helped him scoop away dirt. The dead man lay face down in a shallow grave, over which lumps of mossy earth had been carefully arranged. Lassiter's elbows hiked backward and upward, and the dark broadcloth coat seemed to have been dragged partially away from Lassiter's shoulders.

Sensibly, the two discoverers rummaged around the body only enough to be sure of who lay there. They now yelled loudly several times to summon their companions. When nobody replied, they headed for the turnpike and there assembled others of the search party. These returned and mounted vigil all through the shuddery cold night.

On Sunday morning Hyde County's coroner, Dr. Bryan H. Griffin, arrived with a colleague, Dr. Sanford Long. Under their supervision the body was taken up and bound to a rail, like a dead deer. Two men carried it. The others plied axes to make a trail by which it could be brought to the open.

The doctors found that Clement Lassiter had been shot from a position to his right and a little behind. Several shot had penetrated his right arm, and two of them had ranged on to pierce his heart. Others had reached the lungs and liver. The coroner and his associate decided that Lassiter must have died instantly. They removed several shot that remained lodged in the body, and found them to be of various sizes. Lassiter had been dead for several days, it was hard for even medical experts to say exactly how many.

The Reverend Mr. George Washington Carawan had not joined in the search. Instead he had watched from his yard while others scoured the woods and had appeared nervous. At about supper time of the day when Lassiter was found, Carawan departed from his home. At eleven o'clock that night, he knocked at the door of Henry Tooley, who lived on the Neck Road at Fortescue's Creek near the point where the Pungo River divides Hyde and Beaufort counties.

Presumably the fifty-two-year-old preacher had walked the twelve miles from his own home but seemed deeply anxious to travel yet farther. Tooley launched a canoe in the creek and paddled with Carawan some three miles to the home of Dempsey Lupton on the Pungo. There, at midnight, Carawan asked to be taken across the rive to Durham's Mills.

"When do you want to go?" asked Lupton sleepily.

"Right off now," Carawan replied.

Lupton wanted to wait until morning and offered Carawan a bed in his house. This friendly offer Carawan refused and again urged Lupton to ferry him across at once. Lupton led him to his boat and started across the broad estuary of the Pungo.

Rowing in the dark for a matter of twelve miles, with the running of the tide to complicate matters, took several hours, and it was sunrise before they reached Durham's Mills. As they came near, Carawan volunteered the information that he had so nagged Lupton into a night journey because he, Carawan, was on his way to buy land in Beaufort County.

Others wanted to make the same purchase, he added, and had sent letters ahead.

"Is that your business or your hurry?" inquired Lupton.

"Yes," said Carawan, rather equivocally, and, landing, disappeared into some woods.

If Lupton believed him, his belief lasted no longer than midmorning. Sheriff F. S. Roper of Hyde County arrived at Lupton's with a warrant for Carawan's arrest. Beyond the Pungo, however, he could not trace his man.

Meanwhile, two highly interesting stories were being told broadcast by members of Carwan's household.

The adopted great-nephew, Carawan Sawyer, informed several neighbors that, on the 15th, Lassiter had passed the preacher's dooryard. Shortly afterward, Carawan had headed into the woods as though on a parallel course. In a moment Mrs. Carawan hurried after her husband, carrying a shotgun partially wrapped in her apron.

But more dramatic still was the tale of Seth, a young Negro slave whom Carawan used as a sort of confidential servant. There was little of confidence respected by Seth now, for he said that just before dark on the 15th his master had led him across fields to where, near the road, Lassiter lay dead. Carawan had then ordered Seth to help carry the body into the thick brush and help with its burial. Carawan, said Seth, had also told with a grim face of ambushing Lassiter and shooting him in the back.

By North Carolina law of those days, the testimony of a slave was not admissible as evidence. The Old School Baptists of Rose Bay, however, declined to hamper themselves with such a technicality. They accepted Seth's story, met in solemn session, and disavowed Carawan both as preacher and as member of their church. Handsome apologies were made to the Reverend Mr. Swindell for earlier mistrust.

All these things served as a running start for neighborhood gossip to play havoc with what was left of Carawan's reputation. It was said that he had beaten both of his wives cruelly, that he had made love, stealthily and not unsuccessfully, to several handsome ladies of his congregation, and that he may well have killed three others before ever he aimed his gun at Lassiter.

As for the schoolmaster's murder, it took short time to piece together a motive. Lassiter had boarded with the Carawans for a while before going to Dorset Mason's, and Carawan had picked a quarrel with him in August. When the young man had so risen from his habitual melancholy as to offer fight, Carawan had snatched up his gun and had driven Lassiter from the house. Later, he had brought Mrs. Carawan before a justice of the peace, telling her to swear out a warrant charging Lassiter with attempted rape.

It may be that the justice had heard of Carawan's earlier rantings against his brother Green on a similar charge. At any rate, he called the story fantastic and bade Carawan forget the matter. But Lassiter heard and said that he would sue his accuser for libel in the sum of $2,000. All these things had been more or less hushed up. Now everyone remembered them, recounted them, and embroidered them extravagently.

Unfortunate Mary Carawan, left alone on the farm with late corn to be put in the crib, was given the kindest and most helpful treatment by neighbors, who harvested the crop and otherwise showed sympathy. She is quoted as saying that Carawan's charges against Lassiter were totally unfounded— that the poor dead teacher had "behaved well in the house." She added a plea never to let Carawan hear that she had said so, for he might kill her. Some construed this to mean that she expected him to return, and so he did.

Again it was Seth, the Negro confidential servant, who spread the news. He hurried through a freezing night in January of 1853 to the home of a neighbor. That neighbor ran in turn to summon another neighbor, and others beside. Carawan was back, went the swift word. He had been challenged at his own door, by the barking of his own dog, and Mrs. Carawan had admitted him.

Full thirty farmers, armed and stern, surrounded the house between midnight and dawn and took positions covering every door. At a signal, they entered from all sides and found Carawan talking to his wife. He was in his night clothes and unarmed, and he made no resistance. They allowed him to eat breakfast, and Mrs. Carawan made a bundle of bedding for him. The posse took him in the morning to the jail at Swanquarter.

There he was locked in a brick dungeon beneath the building, a rough cavelike chamber sixteen feet by twenty, with no fireplace or window. The only openings were two barred airholes, and a space in the heavy wooden door through which a bowl of food could be passed. Carawan bore this confinement with a scowling fortitude. He spent much of his time in writing, by candle light. He sent many letters to friends and also worked on what he said was a story of his life. He had finished four hundred pages in the ten months of his imprisonment. This autobiography, could it be traced today, might reveal most interestingly a complex character.

Outside the jail gathered crowds, to curse Carawan's name. On June 2, Carawan addressed to the court, through his attorney, James W. Bryan of New Bern, a plea for change of venue. Judge Mathias E. Manly ordered the case removed to the county of Beaufort for trial at the fall term of court. Carawan was accordingly taken to Washington, where on the morning of November 23 he was brought before Judge John L. Bailey.

His wife appeared with him and his three small sons. Carawan was neatly dressed and seemed in good spirits. He had engaged three notable lawyers to assist James Bryan in his defense. Fenner B. Satterthwaite was a man of commanding appearance, who had studied law while in debtor's prison and who rose to immense legal and political success. William Blount Rodman, small and plump, was a fluent speaker with an encyclopedic law knowledge and had a growing reputation as a state historian. Richard S. Donnell, a former congressman, was also clear-thinking and impressive of aspect.

Against these, Solicitor George S. Stevenson had marshalled two special prosecutors on his own side. Edward J. Warren was perhaps the most celebrated courtroom orator in that part of the state. A native of New England, he was a leader among North Carolina Whigs and later a standard-bearer for secession. His associate in the case, the large-limbed, ruthlessly logical David M. Carter, was to become his law partner.

The state brought thirty witnesses to the stand, to tell of the finding of Lassiter's body, Carawan's flight and his capture. Once Carawan rose to his feet, glaring at a witness. At another time, when someone spoke to his damage, he growled out, "That is false!" and his lawyers gestured for him to hold his peace.

At the end of the second day of the trial, came a diversion that must have been welcome after so much stark talk about strife and death. William Tyson, a Hyde County blacksmith, took the stand to recount a conversation with Carawan. That had been the Friday after Lassiter's disappearance, and three days before his body was discovered. Carawan had mentioned Lassiter, and Tyson had confessed that he had never seen him. Then, as Tyson quoted him, the preacher remarked, "Well, I think it's likely you never will."

Satterthwaite, rising to cross-examine, studied the blacksmith narrowly. "How many drinks have you taken today?" he asked.

"Can't tell," replied Tyson genially.

"Can't you say how many?" Satterthwaite prodded him.

"Well," said Tyson, "I can vouch for two."

This evoked a snicker among the listeners, and Judge Bailey frostily reminded the witness that this was no fit occasion for merriment.

"Don't you consider yourself drunk now?" Satterthwaite pursued his inquiries.

"I think not," said Tyson, but the court was of other opinion.

"Mr. Sheriff, is the witness intoxicated?" demanded Judge Bailey of Beaufort County's sheriff.

"Don't know him, your honor," was that official's understandably cagey reply. Then, plainly seeking to shift responsibility: "The sheriff of Hyde is here."

"The witness is under the influence of liquor," volunteered Sheriff Roper, no doubt speaking from a good acquaintance with Tyson, "but he is not so drunk that he cannot give correct testimony."

"May it please your honor," added Solicitor Stevenson, "I consulted with the sheriff of Hyde before calling the witness on the stand."

These assurances did not satisfy Judge Bailey. "It is evident that the witness is drunk," he pronounced bleakly. "He must be imprisoned till tomorrow at ten o'clock, for contempt of court in coming into court intoxicated."

That concluded the day's session. Tyson was led weaving away, to a cell in the same jail with Carawan. When court re-convened on the following morning he was back on the stand, sober in more senses of the word than one, to repeat his story of Carawan's dark observation about the vanished Lassiter.

The comic aspect of the drama was over. Two more witnesses followed Tyson, giving brief testimony. Then entered the star performer, Carawan Sawyer.

This illiterate young man had never testified before save to the coroner's jury the previous November. For the ordeal at Washington, he primed himself day after day in Washington's bar rooms. But he came to the stand, however, in no such unhappy condition as had the blacksmith Tyson. His story was of the Monday when Lassiter walked past the Carawan farmstead. He told how the preacher had seen his enemy and had gone to the woods, with his wife bringing the shotgun after him. On the day that Lassiter's body was found, said young Sawyer, his great-uncle had drawn him aside for a significant interview. "He said to me," vowed Sawyer, "that if I would say he was home all day on Monday, he would give me the best Negro fellow he had."

Gruellingly Satterthwaite cross-examined the witness. "Weren't you in Asa Paul's shop in Washington yesterday," prompted Satterthwaite, "and didn't you say in the presence of Ruel Jordan, Carney Armstrong and others, that you expected to make more money this week than you had ever made in your life?"

"I don't remember that," said Sawyer stoutly.

"Didn't someone ask you how you'd make it," insisted

Satterthwaite, "and didn't you reply, 'That's best known to myself'?"

"I don't recollect anything like that."

"Didn't you abuse the prisoner's name in the presence of Thomas Bridgman, and say that he ought to be hung?"

"I never said such a thing in my life," flashed back Sawyer. "I am friendly with the prisoner, I have nothing against him and never did have."

All this was damaging enough to Carawan's case, but worse was to befall him when the court met for an evening session after supper. Solomon Northon, jailer at Swanquarter, took the stand and the solicitor handed him two letters. Northon identified them as documents he had found on the floor of Carawan's dungeon, one folded within the other. A. B. Swindell identified their handwriting as Carawan's. Over strenuous objections by defense counsel, the letters were admitted to evidence and read aloud to the jury by Warren. They were supremely worth the hearing.

"MY DEAR OLD FRIEND:—Whether you can get a rogue to leave or not, deliver me. You understand me. You said you had boys that would do thus and thus. Are you going to let them falsely swear me out of my life? You can fix it. I know you can. You see Reuben, he will see you are paid, and so will Bro. Jarvis, for I have directed both of them about the matter, as I have said. Look upon my old gray head, and then look on my poor little babes and my affectionate wife. Brother Jarvis said yesterday from what he knows, or words to this effect, that some on Rose Bay and elsewhere—and gave me to understand that it was A. B. Swindell—said that if it was not for the law, they would go upon Mary, and take her life, because she paid respect for me. Good Lord! Take all these things in consideration, and then deliver me for heaven's sake.

If he will not leave, have done otherwise; for God's sake, let it be done before court in February. Consult Reuben on the subject. And don't delay, for delays breed dangers. You don't live in the neighborhood, therefore you will not be thought of. Oh, deliver me, and never more will I forget you in this life, and I hope the Lord will not in the world to come. Yours. . . ."

"MY DEAR OLD FRIEND:—Do let me know through the channel I have prescribed. Also, let my poor wife know what is the prospect, and she can give me to understand. Tell her to be careful, for they are going to have her sworn; and that is one reason why they have cut her off from me—is for the purpose of setting her against me if they can, and take advantage of her weak mind. Caution her to be on her watch, and not to talk any on the subject, and not to suffer them to question her, and if they try, let her answer be this, "to let that be done on the trial," and stop right there. Don't forget to tell her, if you please. Try to write her a letter in by the lawyers at court, if you cannot get them in by Hoyt, but you can. Get him also to take mine, and I will pay him for you. Tell my wife to give him something, but be sure to do the main thing—to put aside that evidence by hook or by crook. Were you here and suffering as I do now, I would go to death almost, to rescue you. You cannot begin to think how bad it is. I can't tell myself. I have said enough for you to understand me. . . ."

These communications were signed, with rueful humor, "The Old Horse In the Stable."

Carawan had written to his unknown friend "You understand me." Lest others lack understanding, prosecuting counsel stood ready to interpret. Plainly, it was urged, Carawan wanted the damaging evidence of his grand-nephew removed

—by bribery or, failing that, by a more violent method. ". . . boys that would do thus and thus . . . by hook or by crook. . . ." The prosecution closed that same evidence, and on the following day, November 26, the defense announced that it would impeach the testimony of Carawan Sawyer.

Several persons said that Sawyer had told different and less damaging stories about Carawan at the time of the murder, and that during the early days of the trial Sawyer boasted in his cups of money he would make. Only six witnesses spoke for the defense, and in the afternoon David M. Carter delivered the opening argument for the prosecution.

An adjournment until Monday, November 28, and Satterthwaite addressed the jury, though he was ill and sometimes wavered on his feet. He was followed by Stevenson for the state, then by Rodman for the defense. On Tuesday Bryan closed the argument for the prisoner, and that afternoon Warren made the final speech to the jury.

Much had been made by the defense of the fact that only circumstantial evidence had been brought against Carawan, and Warren commented upon this argument with harsh irony.

"We have heard enough eloquence and rhetoric," he said, "and rhetoric and eloquence enough to acquit the prisoner at the bar, if rhetoric and eloquence could avail him. We would suppose that not George W. Carawan, but the state's counsel, the witnesses for the prosecution, and the people of Hyde, were on trial here for high crimes and misdemeanors. . . . But the evidence in this case discloses a murder as foul and atrocious as can be found in the history of crime."

He then proceeded to notice the slurs cast by the defense counsel on circumstantial evidence, both generally and in its specific presentation against Carawan. His remarks were long held in North Carolina to be the classic upholding of that sort of evidence.

"What is circumstantial evidence?" he asked. "It is the evidence of facts, which, according to the course of human experience, usually, and almost invariably accompany an act. . . . If a man commits theft, he does it not in the presence of his fellows. If he commits arson, or burglary, or robbery, he takes no witness with him to testify to the act. If he commits murder, if he coolly and deliberately plots the crime of blood, he seeks to perpetrate the crime where no eye can see him, and where no human sagacity can follow his footsteps. How can he be detected, or brought to answer to justice and the violated law, except by administering the rules of circumstantial evidence?"

This argument he reenforced by reading largely from books of high legal authority, and by reviewing much of the testimony, especially sworn accounts of Carawan's hints about enmity and violence toward Lassiter.

"I trust," he finished, "that you will so perform your duty, as to satisfy both your own consciences and the claims of public justice."

It was now half-past six. Judge Bailey made a brief charge to the jury. He turned his attention to Carawan Sawyer's story and the attacks made upon it by the defense. "You will not convict, gentlemen of the jury, on the testimony of a single tainted witness," he said. "If the matter goes only to his discredit, to his bad character—if his statements out of doors differ from his statements on the stand, the jury will consider the testimony, and give it that weight which it deserves. But if on the stand, in questions pertinent to the issue, he should deny a particular thing, or say that he did not remember when he did remember, and the denial is corrupt, then the witness is guilty of perjury, and the rule is that you must set the whole aside."

These words were sweet in the ears of Carawan's attorneys, and sweetest of all in the ears of Carawan himself. After the jury commenced its deliberations, he went under guard to supper. Elatedly he told his wife, "The jury will acquit me and I will go to Hyde County tomorrow morning on the steamboat."

But an hour passed, and the judge summoned jury, attorneys, and defendant back to the courtroom. He announced that some of the language of his charge might have been misunderstood. He had not intended a flat instruction to disregard Sawyer's testimony, but only a rehearsal of the defense's claims concerning it.

"The prisoner's counsel claim that they have a right to have the testimony of this witness set aside by a stubborn rule of the law," he clarified his earlier remarks and sent the jury back to its room to make up its own mind.

Carawan's spirits sank.

"I shall be condemned tomorrow," he told his wife, "and then they will fasten me up in this place, and you will never be permitted to see me again until I am taken out to be hung."

He asked, and received, permission for his wife and children to spend the night with him in the jail. His wife achieved a make-shift bed for the three little boys. Carawan paced the floor of his dungeon, talking to her on a variety of subjects not subsequently revealed.

In the morning he shaved, and ate the sort of hearty breakfast generally assigned by journalists to persons already condemned. Then he sat down and wrote something on a slip of paper. He handed his spectacles and the inkstand to Mary Carawan.

"Put them away," he directed her, "and be careful not to spill the ink."

She saw the note, folded small, between his fingers. He may have meant for her to take it, too, but did not put it in her hand. It was never seen again. Deputy Sheriff Joseph J. Hinton came to lead him to court.

"Goodbye," he called to other prisoners. "You will never see me again." He also shook the hand of the jailer's wife and turned to leave. He shed a few tears, but dried them before he entered the courtroom.

At 8:30 the jury appeared. Judge Bailey came in shortly after. Carawan sat down behind his attorneys. Not far away Mrs. Carawan took her place, the boys beside her, and began to sob. Solicitor Stevenson and Edward Warren also entered and stood in front of the judge's bench.

"Have you agreed upon a verdict?" the clerk, Mr. Jollie, asked the jury.

"We have," they replied.

"Who shall say for you?" asked Jollie.

Benjamin Patrick, the foreman, rose. Jollie faced the prisoner.

"George Washington Carawan, hold up your right hand," he ordered.

Carawan got to his feet, lifting his hand. He fixed his brilliant eyes upon Patrick.

"Look upon the prisoner, you that have been sworn," Jollie was saying to the jury. "What say you—is he guilty of the felony whereof he stands indicted, or not guilty?"

"Guilty," said Patrick, meeting Carawan's stare.

Carawan sat down, bent forward, and whispered to his lawyers. Bryan rose and asked that the jury be polled. Jollie called the jurors by name.

"Guilty or not guilty?" he asked each in turn; and each replied, "Guilty."

Carawan gazed from juror to juror. As the last of them spoke, he began to unbutton his vest. Jollie swiftly entered the verdict in his records, and spoke once more:

"Gentlemen of the jury, hearken to your verdict as the court has recorded it. You say that George Washington Carawan is guilty of the felony and murder whereof he stands indicted. So say you all."

Judge Bailey then said, "Gentlemen of the jury, you are discharged. The court will take a recess of one hour."

Carawan sprang erect again. From inside his shirt he snatched a single-barrelled pistol—how he had managed to get possession of it in jail, nobody has ever explained. Aiming at Warren, he fired. The courtroom rang with the explosion, and Warren fell sprawling but struggled up again.

Carawan, meanwhile, had drawn another pistol. Hinton, the deputy, sprang to grapple with him. Powerfully Carawan dragged himself free, pushed the muzzle against his own head behind the ear, and again touched trigger. Abruptly he collapsed into his chair, his right arm hanging over the railing and his head sagging forward upon his chest. Blood crimsoned his face and his open shirt front.

Judge Bailey had left the bench. Everyone was shouting and milling. Warren seemed the calmest person there, save only for the silent, slack figure in the prisoner's box. To anxious questions, Warren replied that he was unhurt. The bullet had struck a locket that he wore under his clothes and had glanced away, tearing the stiff padding in his lapel.

Examination proved that Carawan's brain had been pierced from side to side, the bullet lodging just above his left eye. He had died as instantly, perhaps, as had Clement Lassiter. His face, when the blood was sponged from it, seemed quiet and peaceful.

He was buried, appropriately enough, on the spot where once a gallows had stood near the Beaufort County almshouse. Later his relatives brought the body to Rose Bay, where neighbors protested against its burial there. The final grave was dug at Juniper Bay, some miles distant.

The story was told for years that his unquiet spirit walked the shore at that point, and within recent times there were not wanting those who said they believed it.

4

The Corpse in Muddy Creek

BY AUGUST 25, 1914, English and French troops were making a desperate stand along the Marne. The Germans, jaws gaped wide to swallow the Namur forts, counted on Paris as their next morsel. Meanwhile, on the eastern front, Russians drove howling through Prussia, great wild devils led by grand dukes and inspired by the prayers of hairy priests. American newspapers and politicians bade their nation be thankfully neutral, but young adventurers from all forty-eight of the states were heading northward to enlist in Canadian regiments or sailing east to offer themselves to France's Foreign Legion. The European war news overshadowed the opening of the Panama Canal ten days before, the victory of Carranza's forces in Mexico, the frantic rivalry of the New York Yankees and the Boston Braves for first place in the American League, the death of Mrs. Woodrow Wilson in the White House.

But, with most of the gods and saints and phantoms thinking hotly of ways to destroy a world, there must have been at least two smiles in paradise, whence Saint Peter and Izaak Walton are reputed to look down with comradely favor on any man who goes a-fishing. And that is where Julius Crater and H. J. Woody were going on August 25, despite the threat of thunder showers to the west of Winston-Salem in Forsyth County.

Their destination was Muddy Creek near the little village of Clemmons. Bass and bream can be caught there, in turbid waters that range from shallows to fifteen-foot depths. Bamboo poles on their shoulders, they came to the banks of the creek about a hundred yards below the trestle of the Southern Railway.

They baited their hooks and gazed out over the slow brown waters. Downstream at a little distance, Crater saw something white. A floating handkerchief, perhaps? The two men ambled nearer. The object hung on the surface about fifteen feet from the bank. One of the fishermen stepped out on some rocks and probed with the butt of his pole.

It was no handkerchief. Another hoisting poke, and the thing stirred and shifted in the muddy water. It was a man's naked body, and the man had been dead for a long time.

With shaky hands, Crater and Woody dragged their ghastly find nearer. One dead leg trailed a piece of broken cast iron, tied on with rope at the knee. Another weight, apparently larger, slipped away from lashings at the dead man's shoulder and sank from sight. Whoever had put the body into Muddy Creek had not wanted it to be found.

Far off somewhere in the hot silent air wailed a train whistle. At once both anglers raced for the railway trestle upstream, and reached it in time to wave frantically at the approaching freight train. The engineer, a man named Frazier, clapped on his brakes and slid to a halt. He listened to the story, then hurried on to Winston-Salem, where he telephoned to Coroner William N. Dalton. That capable officer hurried out, in a cranky car of the era, gathering help on the way.

Dragged up on dry land, the body proved to be badly decomposed. Coroner Dalton saw that the face had been battered in. The jaw was broken and the skull fractured behind the right ear. Several teeth were missing, and a cord around the neck looked like the lash of a buggy whip. In life the poor fellow had been lean and tall, and apparently young.

With the help of his companions, the coroner dug a grave at the creek side for temporary protection of the grisly find. On the following day, under supervision of Sheriff G. W. Flynt, it was dug up again and placed in the keeping of Frank Vogler, an undertaker. Sheriff Flynt caused a gold-crowned tooth to be detached, for possible later identification. Coroner Dalton conducted an inquest on the spot, and the jury brought in a verdict that "the deceased came to his death by some cause at the hands of some person or persons to the jury unknown."

So long submerged, that rotted and battered corpse would be hard to identify. Neither sheriff nor police officers had record of a recent disappearance in or near Winston-Salem. The county commissioners announced a reward of $200 for the arrest and conviction of the murderer, and a number of detectives, professional and amateur, came to Vogler's undertaking establishment to try to identify the body.

Among those who came to Vogler's were several members of the track crew of the Norfolk and Western Railroad. One of these thought the body resembled in some ways a fellow track-layer, G. J. Warren, who had left his job August 17. He told Police Chief J. A. Thomas, who called on Warren's wife, proprietor of the Piedmont Boarding House on Liberty Street near the courthouse square.

Ida Ball Warren was sometimes cited as proof of the proverb that those who kick the highest often settle down the hardest. She was one of a numerous family that had grown up on a farm not greatly distant from where the body had been pulled out of Muddy Creek. A surviving photograph reveals that she was stockily-built, flat-faced, and coarse-featured— even if that portrait did her less than justice, hers was never the face to launch a thousand ships. Nevertheless, she possessed some sort of attraction. One man, at least, was to suggest that her charm partook of the occult.

In any case, literally scores of young men came calling. Some of them she must have admired greatly. In 1899, when she was twenty-two years old, she gave birth to a daughter, Pearl, whose father never was positively named.

In 1908, she captivated a railroad worker named Sam Christy, a lean, long-faced youngster eight years her junior. He deserted his wife and three children to run off with Ida. Mrs. Christy divorced him, and no word came from the elopers for four years. Then, in November of 1912, she reappeared in Winston-Salem. She was now the wife of G. J. Warren, a rather saturninely handsome and soberly courteous Louisianan with brilliant eyes and a waxed moustache like the villains in old-fashioned melodramas. They leased the Piedmont Boarding House, which Mrs. Warren operated while her husband worked as a section hand for the Norfolk and Western. In March, 1914, Ida Warren's fifteen-year-old daughter Pearl married Clifton Stonestreet, a collector for a furniture company.

This family seemed a solid, even-tempered, respectable one, for all the earlier irregular escapades of Ida. Now she told Chief Thomas that her husband had gone to Louisiana to pay his sick mother a visit.

The body was buried at last and seemingly forgotten for months. It was late in March, 1915, that the chief of police received a letter from a Mrs. Warren in Louisiana. This lady wondered what had happened to her son, who lived in Winston-Salem and had not written to her since midsummer. His initials were G. J., and could Chief Thomas help her locate him?

On April 1, the chief again called at the Piedmont Boarding House, with the letter and with questions. The agitation of Ida Ball Warren gave the experienced officer strongly to suspect that locating G. J. Warren could be accomplished at no greater distance than to a certain unmarked grave in the cemetery. He conferred with Sheriff Flynt, also with Dave Knott, the crisp foreman under whom Warren had worked. Yet again, on April 7, the body was dug up for Knott to study. He looked thoughtfully at long legs, exceptionally high insteps, and a wen at the back of the head. These things, he said, induced him positively to identify the body as that of G. J. Warren.

Flynt and Thomas repaired together on the following day to the Piedmont Boarding House. Mrs. Warren refused to answer their new questions and was taken to the county jail, where she was locked up on a charge of murder. On April 9 she sent for the sheriff and said that she had something to tell him.

"Tell me now," he urged.

"I just can't begin," she demurred, but gathered resolution. "Mr. Flynt, you are right," she said. "That man killed Mr. Warren."

"What man?" asked the sheriff, who did not know what she was talking about.

"Christy. They had a terrible fight in the room."

"What time was this?"

"About four o'clock. I did not hear anything of the fight. I was in the kitchen."

Of all this incoherent jabber, one name struck a responsive chord in the sheriff's mind. Christy . . . Flynt had been making inquires lately, and he remembered that Christy was the young railroader with whom Ida Ball had fled in 1908. Under Flynt's persistent questions, the prisoner filled in the story.

She and Christy had lived together as Mr. and Mrs. S. P. Kearns, first in Virginia, then at Grand Saline, Texas. At Grand Saline, Ida had operated a boarding house and had yielded to the trim moustache and consequential good manners of a boarder named G. J. Warren. Captivating but conservative, Warren urged her to quit her irregular relationship with Christy and go back to her girlhood home and marry him. This she consented to do, leaving both Christy and the boarding house without saying goodbye but taking along some $800 Christy had saved and stored in his bedroom. Pearl, her daughter, came with the couple to Winston-Salem where, on the day of their arrival, they had been married in the office of the register of deeds.

Christy, pursuing, vanished again when he found that his beloved had married Warren. But early on the morning of August 18, 1914, he was back and came to the Piedmont Boarding House.

"Christy came in the bedroom about four o'clock and choked Mr. Warren to death with a rope," she told the sheriff. "After choking him, Christy put him in a trunk and dragged it into Room Number 14. I was in the kitchen at the time."

This melodramatic violence, according to Ida Warren, was then matched with cool practicality. Christy went out, found two colored men on the street and brought them back to help him drag the trunk downstairs, where they loaded it on a hired wagon.

"Mister, you must have gold in this trunk," Ida heard one of the helpers say, and felt that she would faint with suspense and horror. Christy drove off, she continued her story, and returned later in the evening. He told her that he had driven all day through the streets of Winston-Salem, then went to Muddy Creek after dark, tied chunks of iron to the body and sank it in the creek. He said that he had taken the trunk to the home of Clifton Stonestreet, Ida's son-in-law.

Then, she said, Christy had asked her to go with him to "some unknown place where we would never be found" and insisted that he could take care of her. She refused to leave, and he remained at the Piedmont Boarding House until September. Then, she said, she had begged him to leave and he did so. He had written to her from Grand Saline, under his old alias of S. P. Kearns. She had answered the letter, she said, but had never heard from him.

Chief Thomas telegraphed officers in Grand Saline and neighboring towns, asking that Christy be arrested. He then sought out Clifton Stonestreet and put him in jail.

Stonestreet denied having helped in any way to dispose of his wife's stepfather. His first knowledge of the crime, he earnestly declared, came when Christy appeared at the Stonestreet home on Sixth Street and remarked casually, "Well, I have got shed of him."

Stonestreet asked who he meant, and Christy replied, "Warren." He then told a story, according to Stonestreet, much like that of Ida Warren—he had driven here and there with the body in the trunk until, after dark, he had gone to the creek and sunk it by means of weights. Some days later,

Stonestreet told the officers, Christy had left Winston-Salem, commenting that he could find no work there.

But Stonestreet's efforts to sound detached and only slightly involved in these exciting matters were notably impeded when a digging party in his basement turned up the smashed remains of a trunk and partially burned fragments of clothing which were identified as Warren's.

Thus April 9 had produced two stories pointing to Christy as Warren's murderer. On April 10, Chief Thomas received a telegram from Grand Saline, informing him that Christy was under arrest there.

The chief and the sheriff left for Texas on April 12, armed with extradition papers. Two days later they were on their way back with Christy. Fully 150 citizens of Grand Saline saw the train off, most of them calling out good wishes to the prisoner.

Silently Christy rode with his captors for most of the night. At four o'clock in the morning, as the train approached Chattanooga, he informed Sheriff Flynt that he wanted to talk.

Talk he did, and much to the point. He told of his romance with Ida Ball. Her powers of fascination, he suggested, bordered on the hypnotic. "I became a perfect slave to her," he said, describing their flight together, their various home-makings, and the coming of Warren.

"Then the whole trouble started," he said plaintively. "Ida Ball apparently tired of me and took up with this man. I knew it, yes, but what could I do? I was not legally married and was in her power deeper than I really thought at the time, I guess."

Ida's flight to Winston-Salem and her marriage to Warren followed. Christy returned to Grand Saline and married "a fine little woman," a girl who had been a chum of Ida's daughter Pearl. Then he began to get letters from Ida.

"... she urged and begged me to come back to her," he told Flynt. "My wife got hold of one of these letters." Christy smiled over the memory, broadly but not happily. "Finally I decided to come up and see what Ida wanted."

He found out, after several stealthy visits to the Piedmont Boarding House and some equivocation on the part of the woman who had called him to her from so far away.

"She wanted me to get rid of Warren. She said he was beating and abusing her and she wanted him out of the way. I asked her why she didn't get some officers when he was beating her up and she said if she had him arrested he would tell all about her past life and about her living with me in Texas."

The force of this argument came home strongly to Christy, he declared, and he listened seriously to Ida's alternative proposal. The plot to murder Warren was "hatched," as Christy put it, at Stonestreet's house. Stonestreet, according to Christy, had quarrelled with Warren before marrying Ida's daughter and the two men had not spoken since. As Christy told of the murder, it happened in a vastly different fashion from that described by Ida and by Stonestreet.

"On the morning of August 18, at about four o'clock—I wasn't there—Mrs. Warren, as prearranged for the first opportunity, placed some chloroform on a handkerchief and held it under Warren's nose as he slept in the bed beside her. Then she arose and called Stonestreet, her son-in-law. He took a rope and strangled the man to death. Then they placed the body in a trunk. I was called about eight o'clock that morning and told by Stonestreet that 'the———is gone now.' "

In published accounts of Christy's narrative, Stonestreet's alleged description of Warren is always indicated by what Booth Tarkington has termed a chaste dash. Whatever Stonestreet may have said, it made sense to Christy:

"I knew what he meant. He asked me to get a hack and help him take the body away."

Later that day, continued Christy, he and Stonestreet took the trunk, by hired wagon, to Muddy Creek. There, after dark they removed the body. Stonestreet, Christy added, smashed Warren's face with a short-handled axe, remarking, "Well, they won't be able to recognize him now." The body was then weighted and pushed into the water.

So ended Christy's narrative, which must have sounded shudderingly impressive when told by the dim lights of a trundling car.

At midnight on April 16 the train reached the station at Winston-Salem, and Sheriff Flynt and Chief Thomas looked out at a huge and close-packed mob of people—more than two thousand of them, the officers estimated. They slipped out with Christy on the far side of the train and hurried to the county jail, where they mustered a special guard.

Inside the jail, Christy and Stonestreet were brought face to face.

"This is a pretty predicament you've all gotten me into," Christy greeted the other.

"I haven't gotten you anywhere," said Stonestreet glumly.

"Why didn't you tell the whole thing?" Christy scolded at him. "Why did you tell all you knew on me and not tell anything you did?"

"I did not know anything about it," growled Stonestreet.

"Cliff, you know you went with me to Muddy Creek, and

you rolled the body into the creek." said Christy. "You also hit Warren in the face with an axe."

"Who sawed the handle off the axe?" demanded Stonestreet.

"I'm not talking about that," Christy said impatiently, as though brushing aside an unimportant detail.

"I don't know a damn thing about it," persisted Stonestreet. "The old lady told it all."

On April 22 a preliminary hearing was called. Stonestreet and Christy were brought in, handcuffed together. Ida Ball Warren entered the courtroom separately, and a reporter said that she chewed gum unconcernedly. She spoke to Pearl, who was present, carrying her bright-eyed, six-months-old daughter. It was a hot day, and electric fans hummed in the room.

Each of the three defendants had separate counsel. Attorneys Fred Parrish and J. Gilmer Korner represented Christy. E. B. Jones and John Clement appeared for Mrs. Warren, and Frank Baldwin for Stonestreet.

The room was crammed with curious spectators, who were chided by the court for applauding the various witnesses. Once or twice Mrs. Warren was observed to laugh at testimony of Chief Thomas. At the end of the hearing, all three defendants were ordered back to jail, to await trial at the July term of Superior Court.

On July 29, a grand jury returned a true bill charging the three with murder, and an extra count against Stonestreet, charging him with being an accessory after the fact. On the next morning the defendants appeared in court with their lawyers. Ida Warren wore a blue percale dress and a large picture hat, and seemed nervous. All three pleaded not guilty. Judge E. P. Cline granted a motion for change of venue, and ordered that jurymen be brought from Rockingham County to hear the evidence.

On August 4 the trial began. "By eight o'clock in the morning," wrote an observer, "the streets around the court house square and Main Street, leading to the jail, were crowded with men, women and children, black and white, all hoping to catch a glimpse of the noted prisoners as they were led from the jail to the court house."

With no sympathy for the hopes of the crowd, Sheriff Flynt smuggled the prisoners out of the rear door of the jail and through a side entrance of the courthouse. A crowd so overflowed the courtroom that Judge Cline had to order the doorway cleared so that the jury could enter.

Stonestreet and Christy were clean shaven and neatly dressed. Their appearance was called "pleasing" by a newspaper reporter. Ida Warren seemed even fashionable, with a white lace collar to her blue dress and a large dark blue hat trimmed with purple flowers. She chewed gum, as at the preliminary hearing. Stonestreet and Christy sat on either side of her, and behind them sixteen-year-old Pearl Stonestreet held her baby and wept softly.

Julius Crater, Coroner W. N. Dalton, David Knott, Chief Thomas, and Sheriff Flynt were among the first witnesses for the prosecution. The conflicting and damaging statements of the defendants were retold, despite frantic objections from the defense attorneys. Very little of the testimony was appetizing, though most of it was important. Ida Warren's sister, Mrs. William Henning, spoke for the state to say that Ida had told her, "I planned that murder."

There was one laugh, heartily enjoyed. Police Officer T. B. Smothers took the stand to say that he had seen Ida Warren and Christy meeting frequently at the Stonestreet home. Attorney Parrish rose to cross-examine.

"Some folks said you killed that man when the body was found, didn't they?" asked Parrish.

"Some folks said Sheriff Flynt, Chief Thomas and Jailer J. J. Adams killed him," replied Smothers, and His Honor rapped loudly to discourage the merriment.

On the second day of the trial appeared the most sensational witness and the most eccentric, a dolefully funny young woman with the odd name of Lummy Davis. Lummy had been in jail under a charge of vagrancy while the accused murderers were there and had been allowed to walk about the hallway.

"Did you ever say anything to Mrs. Warren about the murder?" asked Solicitor Porter Graves.

"I did," replied Lummy. "I said to her, why did you all kill him?"

"What was her reply?"

"She said: 'I knew what was best for me and who does for me.' "

"While you were in the jail did you hear any conversation between Christy and Mrs. Warren?"

The five defense lawyers leaned forward as one man to listen. It developed that Lummy most assuredly had heard such a conversation. Standing behind a corner in the jail, she had heard Ida Warren and Christy talking. Ida urged Christy to swear that he had killed Warren in self-defense, after Warren had drawn a gun.

Like Ann Butler who testified against Ann Simpson in Fayetteville sixty-five years before, Lummy Davis was now in for the most embarrassing of cross-examinations. Vigorously Attorney Parrish questioned her, forcing her to admit a variety of disreputable adventures. Poor Lummy wept loudly on the stand, and even the attorneys for the prisoners seemed to pity her.

The defense opened its case on Friday, August 12. Christy's lawyers said they would call no witnesses, and Attorney Baldwin presented several character witnesses to swear to their good opinion of Stonestreet. Then:

"Ida Ball Warren, come around and be sworn," said Judge Jones.

She rose, visibly nervous and pale-faced. She spoke slowly, but with growing confidence and distinctness.

On the night before the murder, she said, Christy had come to the Piedmont Boarding House and had been hidden by her in Room 14. On the next morning, she had risen between 4:30 and 5:00, had gone to this room and awakened Christy. Shortly afterward, Warren had appeared at the door, a pistol in his hand, to find her in Christy's arms.

Warren's reaction, as Ida described it, was the traditional one of a jealous husband with a weapon. "You ———, what are you doing in here?" he roared. "I'll kill you." Again the published account affords a Tarkingtonian chaste dash. Christy, said Ida, caught Warren's pistol hand and grappled with him, while she ran out and into the kitchen. Shortly afterward, Christy came to tell her that he had killed Warren by striking him with a monkey wrench. How this tool had come so conveniently to Christy's hand in Room 14 of the Piedmont Boarding House was not explained.

The rest of Ida's story agreed with what she had told Sheriff Flynt at the time of her arrest.

On cross-examination, she said that she had kept silent about her husband's death through fear of Christy and the police. Warren, she said, had treated her kindly and had provided for her abundantly, but now he was dead. "I was afraid that I would get myself into trouble," she explained, thereby becoming a candidate for the late Alexander Woollcott's projected gallery of experts at understatement. "And I knew that I was guilty of being in the room with Christy."

Arguments to the jury followed Ida's testimony. The lawyers completed their addresses shortly before nine o'clock that evening. The three prisoners ate supper in a chamber adjoining the courtroom and waited. At eleven o'clock they were led back. The jury filed in and sat down. Foreman J. F. Fulton rose when called upon by the clerk.

"We find the defendants, Ida Ball Warren and Samuel P. Christy, guilty of murder in the first degree," announced Fulton, "and the defendant, Clifton Stonestreet, guilty of being an accessory after the fact."

The crowd had never left the courtroom, and every eye was fixed upon the three prisoners. Ida Warren seemed to face disaster with untrembling defiance. Christy looked around for a cuspidor and spat tobacco juice into it. Stonestreet appeared as flinty as his name. After a moment he sighed, as though relieved. Judge Cline, after conferring with Stonestreet's attorney, pronounced upon Stonestreet a prison sentence of three years.

Judge Jones spoke in protest against the verdict. So did Fred Parrish. They gave notice of appeal to the Supreme Court.

"It is a complicated case," said Judge Cline. "I don't feel sure of myself from a legal standpoint. I have not had time to prepare words in which to sentence the two defendants, except as provided by the statute. The verdict is a terrible conclusion to a case where a man and woman try to reach out to each other across the grave of another man."

He paused. Apparently he was deeply moved.

"The court," he said, "cannot say what the Court of Appeals will do. It may grant you another trial. But in the meantime, if I were you I would think more seriously of the situation confronting you now, for if a new trial is not granted you, your lives will be forfeited."

He looked straight at Ida Warren and Samuel Christy, who stood side by side before him.

"I will not make your ordeal longer," he continued, "but I want you to realize something of the ordeal of the court in being forced to pronounce the extreme penalty of the law upon a woman."

One more pause. Finally:

"It is the judgment of this court that you and each of you shall be conveyed to the state penitentiary at Raleigh, where, on Friday, September 24, you will be electrocuted and killed with electricity. And may God have mercy on your souls."

The clock struck midnight, resoundingly mournful, as the prisoners were led back to jail.

Young Pearl Stonestreet said farewell to her husband and mother. Throughout the trial she had sat with them. Plainly unconnected with the crime, blameless for any of the shabby events connected with it, she had appeared as the most loyal and affectionate of wives, daughters, and mothers. Now she sought shelter with her father-in-law, an honest and painfully grieving carpenter.

Attorneys for both Christy and Ida Warren presented appeals to the State Supreme Court. A stay of sentence was granted as the justices delayed decision until the fall term of court.

Justice Walter M. Clark wrote the opinion, in which his colleagues concurred unanimously. Step by step he reviewed the evidence, one by one he disposed of the protests of the defense. With chill determination he refused to deprive Ida Warren of her melancholy celebration as the first woman to be sent to North Carolina's electric chair. After four decades, his words still tingle:

"Upon the evidence she seems to have been the moving spirit in the murder, the veritable Lady Macbeth of the tragedy.... Upon the record the husband of the prisoner, Warren, was put to death by his wife and her paramour by a preconcerted, predetermined murder, cold blooded and relentless, without any mitigating or extenuating circumstances.

"We find no error in the conduct of the case by the learned judge, and the twelve jurors have founded their verdict upon competent evidence which justified their conclusions."

That should be emphatic enough for anyone, it would seem. A new date was set for execution of the sentence, March 21, 1916. The convicted murderers were sent to state prison at Raleigh.

March brought to Verdun in France a blood-boltered battle of desperate armies, to various National Guard units orders for mobilization and advance to the Mexican border, and to the desk of Governor Locke Craig a deluge of letters. Literally hundreds of North Carolinians pleaded that mercy be shown to Ida Ball Warren. On March 20, Attorney Cameron Morrison led Ida's brother, Ed Ball, to the governor's office. Ball said that he considered his sister mentally incompetent and unable to comprehend the enormity of her crime.

Morrison, only five years away from the governorship, added to this a suit for mercy that smacked of the great legal-oratory days of Fenner Bryan Satterthwaite and Warren Winslow. "I can't conceive," he rose to a quivering climax, "of the leader of North Carolina's knighthood and chivalry allowing a poor, wretched, unhappy woman to die on the gallows on the pretext that it is necessary to law and order in North Carolina."

In his eloquent fervor, Morrison evidently forgot that the gallows had been superseded in North Carolina by the electric chair, full six years previously; forgot, too, that J. G. Warren was just as dead as though his destruction had been planned and procured by the most coarsely and unsympathetically male of murderers.

Governor Craig listened mutely and expressionlessly, forbearing to remind Morrison of either of these matters. At the end of the hearing, the governor announced that he felt unable to commute the sentence. When Morrison and Ball had left, Craig sat alone, and perhaps the silence softened his mood. He issued a new statement, commuting the two death sentences to life imprisonment. Plainly Morrison's impassioned argument had had its effect, for Craig's words sound like an echo of Morrison's:

"I cannot contemplate with approval that this woman, unworthy and blackened by sin though she be, shall be shrouded in the cerements of death, dragged along the corridor, and bound in the chair of death."

Christy and Ida stayed in prison until 1930, when both were paroled—Ida on May 31, Christy on August 11. Stonestreet had been released long before and had been welcomed home by his tragic, faithful young wife.

Today they may all be alive. If so, surely no great matter of justice or information would be served by trying to find out where they live, or how, or under what names.

Some discussion and argument has prevailed through the years as to which of the various stories of Warren's death was the true one. Christy, it will be remembered, said that Ida had called him from Texas to kill her husband, had conducted the discussion as to approved methods, and finally had assigned the job to Stonestreet. Stonestreet, in his turn, pictured himself as a sort of outsider, with only a mild interest in the affair, and laid the blame on Christy. Ida told two stories, differing slightly in detail, but agreeing that Christy had fought with Warren and struck him dead while she hid herself in another room.

On the basis of all evidence presented at the trial, there was some truth in each story, and deceit as well. Ida Warren convinced nobody when she claimed to be amazed and frightened at what befell her husband. Chief Justice Clark, in comparing her to Lady Macbeth, and Samuel Christy, in calling himself her hypnotized slave, spoke vividly and understandably of Ida Ball Warren. It is reasonably certain that she wrote asking Christy to come, and when he arrived she would hardly turn to someone else for the favor of killing Warren. She emerges as the planner, Christy as the actual slayer, and Stonestreet as the sympathetic helper in the disposing of Warren's body.

Time heals all wounds, even those dealt to the nerves. Fishermen still drop baited hooks into Muddy Creek. But, if we are to believe Forsyth County people, nobody is over-zealous in the investigation of enigmatic-seeming objects that may float offshore. Indeed, several timid anglers are reputed to have walked quickly away from dubious half-submerged things, to fish somewhere else—even in another creek than the one called Muddy.

5

Where Are You, Kenneth Beasley?

THE KIDNAPPING OF A child, whether for profit or for revenge, deals cruelly and despicably in the souls' agony of parents and child alike. It demands in its perpetrator a special depravity and heartlessness. Its infamy shocks a community and a nation, and seemingly the shock cannot wear off. In Currituck County, North Carolina's northeasternmost corner, the pathetic memory of little Kenneth Beasley chills after half a century, and the chill may linger there through generations to come.

Currituck County is a strip of the Outer Banks and the mainland coast and the sound. In 1905 as now, the population was about 6,000, mostly rural folk with understandable pride in themselves. Currituck County's patriotic young men had fought well in two wars, helping to win one and lose the other. Its residents were farmers, fishermen, and lumber-cutters. The black peaty soil was fruitful in potatoes, melons, beans, and corn, and the forests of oak and cedar had not as yet been cut over. Thomas Jarvis of Jarvisburg, the preacher's son who had taught himself law and had risen to become

North Carolina's governor, minister to Brazil, and United States senator, was Currituck's most distinguished native son, alive or dead. And Mr. Samuel M. Beasley, a prosperous farmer, was serving his second term in the State Senate, with neighborly predictions of big political things to come.

"Beautiful," people said of the Beasley farm just south of the little crossroads community of Poplar Branch, midway down Currituck County's shoreline. It was well-worked, hospitable, homelike, and cheerful. Mrs. Beasley, the former Miss Carrie Walker, was a gentle, accomplished woman. Her sons were Moran, seventeen years old, and Kenneth, eight. The third and youngest child was a daughter, four-year-old Ethel. Beasley himself was a middle-sized man with strong, handsome features. He wore a heavy fair moustache and shielded his near-sighted blue eyes with spectacles.

From all accounts, Kenneth was good-looking, too. He was small for his age, with slim hands and feet, blond hair and wide blue eyes like his father's. Probably he had the appearance and manner of a sensitive, thoughtful child. He was doing well in the third grade at the two-teacher Poplar Branch School conducted in the Odd Fellows' Hall a quarter of a mile from home. Possibly he was interested in the thrilling flight of the Wright brothers, two years before at Kitty Hawk in Dare County to the south. He may even have played at pioneer aviation with his cousin Benny Walker and his chums, Ernest Wright and Edward Meggs, who lived on neighboring farms.

Miss Nina Harrison, who with tall, lean Professor M. P. Jennings taught the Poplar Branch School, was to say for publication that she dearly loved her pupil Kenneth; but others of Miss Nina's family were not so well disposed toward the Beasleys.

Those Harrisons were an aggressive breed. Joshua Harrison was a man in his fifties, six feet tall, with a grizzled beard and an incandescent temper. In earlier years he had twice been accused of homicide, but both times the courts had cleared him. His prosperous farm lay near Jarvisburg, a good five miles west of Poplar Branch, and sometime in the middle 1870's he had married Miss Anna Jarvis, a favorite younger sister of the able Currituckan who became governor and senator. He had three grown sons, Hoje, Joe, and Thomas, who helped him work the farm. His older daughter, Mrs. Anna Harrison Gallop, operated a lodging house in Norfolk, Virginia, and his younger daughter was, as we have seen a teacher.

Joshua Harrison supplemented his income from the farm's produce by operating a lively enterprise in one of his barns— for years he had sold wine, to the loud relish of some neighbors and to the frank disapproval of others. One customer, T. N. Davenport, would swear in a court of law that it was "good wine." But Sam Beasley disagreed with this judgment, and in 1903, largely through Senator Beasley's efforts, the legislature passed a bill declaring the sale of wine illegal in Currituck.

Harrison and Beasley had discussed this legislation against wine during October of 1904, when they met on the road between their farms. Harrison began with scowling accusations. "I hear that 1903 legislation was for me," he said threateningly.

Beasley, smaller and calmer, was not afraid. "If you heard that," he replied evenly, "you heard right; for you are the only person in Currituck creating a disturbance, and the people petitioned the legislature on the subject."

Harrison's smouldering temper flared up. "I'll be damned if I don't sell it in spite of 'em," he vowed furiously. "If I can't sell it in gallons I'll sell it in barrels, and the people can come and get it. When they stop me from selling it they'll be God damned sorry for it."

Understandably, the two did not speak to each other again for some months following.

The following February was cold in Currituck County. Senator Beasley attended the session of the legislature in Raleigh but returned briefly on February 8, a Wednesday. Frozen snow lay on the ground, and on Friday he saw Kenneth dress for school in a heavy gray suit, a blue cap, and stout brown stockings of country knit. Kenneth had a new two-bladed pocket knife that his father had never seen before.

On the following morning, Senator Beasley left before dawn on his long cold return trip to Raleigh, and Kenneth had not risen from bed in time to bid his father goodbye.

Monday, February 13, was a school day again. Kenneth trudged off in his brown stockings, blue cap, and gray suit, with a heavy overcoat and gloves. "I've seen some mighty pretty puppies," he called out to his mother as he left, "and I want one."

If Mrs. Beasley watched her son, she could have followed his progress almost all the way to the Odd Fellows' Hall at the crossroads.

The hall stood where the road that today is State Highway 3 came to the rough, narrow Sound Road. To the north could be seen several country homes, in clearings among thick woods, and Poplar Branch flowed across the Sound Road and into the ocean. Beyond the houses stood Wilson Woodhouse's store where the country post office was kept, and, fronting all this, the broad, salty waters of Currituck Sound. Miss Nina Harrison, who taught the four lower grades, marked Kenneth present. He pulled off his slush-soaked shoes and dried his feet at the schoolroom stove. That morning he was called upon several times for recitation. As the sun came out, the air warmed, and Kenneth went out for noon recess without his overcoat. When the bell rang for afternoon classes, at 1 P.M., he did not return.

Kenneth's cousin, Benny Walker, was able to say that he had played with Kenneth at noon and that, when the bell rang, Kenneth had turned toward the woods behind the hall. "I'm going back farther," he said, and that was the last Benny saw of him.

This dereliction of a good pupil seemed to amaze Miss Harrison, who reported to Professor Jennings. A glance into the cloakroom revealed Kenneth's overcoat hanging there, with gloves in its pocket. Had the boy meant to play truant, would he have left his overcoat? The schoolmaster sent Everett Wright to go and look for Kenneth. Everett did so, and returned to say he had found nothing. Professor Jennings then dispatched Benny Walker, with orders to make a careful search.

Cold rain began to fall as young Benny left the hall, but he made a businesslike search of the woods. Then he returned to the Sound Road and sturdily tramped half a mile to Woodhouse's store, arriving at about two o'clock. The stocky proprietor had not seen the vanished boy and immediately recognized the arrival of an emergency. He locked up his store, returned to the hall with Benny, and urged that school be dismissed at once, in order to make a systematic search.

Jennings began to organize parties of the older boys, while Woodhouse hurried to summon neighbors who were experienced hunters and knew the swampy timberland well.

The temperature dropped, degree by degree, and by late afternoon the rain had changed to snow. At four o'clock, fully a hundred and fifty searchers had gathered. They began to explore the dank, gloomy clumps and thickets. It was a stubborn effort, and ranged for miles. But midnight came, and no possible trace of little Kenneth had been turned up.

Mrs. Beasley had been notified, and her older son, Moran, was in the search party. On the following morning, February 14, Sam Beasley was handed a telegram as he sat in the hall of the State Senate, and no more doleful valentine could have been sent or received. He left at once, to go home by train and carriage, and arrived after midnight.

Another search had taken place that day, back and forth across miles of swamp. W. A. Doxery, a man familiar with the wilderness, was a leading spirit. He crept on hands and knees under low bridges and waded to his waist in icy water. On Wednesday, February 15, Beasley joined in the throngs who by now were organized for a more systematic hunt.

As many as three hundred men and boys formed a line, with intervals of eight feet, and drew their formation like a half-mile dragnet through one section of woods, then another. Hunting dogs were brought, but rain and snow had soaked the ground and they could not pick up a trail. By now many were saying that little Kenneth must have become lost and would be dead by now from the cold. Wise huntsmen's eyes turned to the leaden sky, squinting after the telltale swoop of buzzards. But on that night came from somewhere a rumor that a child had been crying for help from a deep-thicketed lumberman's cabin.

By dawn, searchers beat their way to that cabin, which was said to be occupied by a recluse—a "foreigner," said some, a "Yankee," said others. Whatever his origin, he was gone. Other parties began to visit and search houses.

On February 24, the Raleigh *News and Observer* carried on its front page a one-word headline:

KIDNAPPED?

The story itself was in the main a quotation from a letter, written to "a gentleman of Raleigh" by "a resident of Currituck County." Neither sender nor recipient were identified, then or later when this interesting piece of publication was a focus of legal comment. It said in part:

"There was a strange man seen up about Barco postoffice and two more places by three different men. He was in a buggy drawn by a black mule and had the boy down between his knees, but the people saw him before they heard that the boy was missing. These men say that saw him that the boy was crying and seemed dissatisfied, but the man was talking to him rough."

If the names of the gentleman of Raleigh and the resident of Currituck County were omitted, other names were offered as witnesses to the buggy and the captive boy—W. E. Ansell, Caleb Barco, and Jack Griggs. Finally:

"Mr. Joshua Harrison went on Tuesday morning and never got back until Sunday. He claimed he had been to Pasquotank."

The reader was left to a rather pointed conclusion.

Two days later, on Sunday, February 26, the *News and Observer* announced that the search in Currituck had been abandoned and that the whole community was convinced that Kenneth was in the hands of kidnappers. One rumor said that he was held prisoner near Shiloh, in neighboring Camden County. At the end of the column of news and surmise was included a statement by his teacher, Nina Harrison. "His was a fine and lovely character," she said, "never hard to control but gentle and lovely as a girl. He loved dearly to go to school and always tried hard to master his studies, which he did successfully, and to please his teacher, who was so fond of him, and whose disappearance from her room has so saddened her heart."

This was a touching tribute, even if the syntax was somewhat shaky for a schoolmistress. On the same day that it appeared, to be read widely throughout North Carolina, Joshua Harrison hitched his dark-skinned mule to his buggy and went calling at the Beasley home, with Miss Nina at his side.

The young teacher spoke first, inquiring after the health of Mrs. Beasley. She was told that the lady had collapsed and was under sedatives, now and then moaning, "Give me the body of my boy." Then Harrison addressed Senator Beasley for the first time since their dispute about the wine legislation.

"Did you see the article in the *News and Observer?*" he inquired.

Beasley replied that he had.

"Do you believe it?" asked Harrison. "It's a batch of lies. I want you to write to the paper and say it was a lie. If your son was kidnapped some of the neighbors did it."

Beasley said, probably with considerable effort to keep his voice steady, that he had not written the letter to the gentleman of Raleigh, and he would not bother the editors of the *News and Observer.*

"I can prove where I was Monday and Tuesday and the remainder of the week," Harrison assured him, and drove away.

Beasley did not seem to take seriously, at first, the hints that Harrison may have carried off his son. He went to Shiloh in a fruitless effort to pick up Kenneth's trail. When his neighbors abandoned the search, he and his son Moran roamed day after day through the silent winter woods. They explored brush piles and plumbed stagnant pools. They found nothing.

But in March the Beasleys had a visitor, Mr. J. J. Pierce of Shiloh. Pierce had heard of the vanished boy and of Beasley's visit to his home town. He, Pierce, had seen Kenneth once, three years earlier, at church at Poplar Branch. And on another Sunday, March 5, he had thought he saw Kenneth again —on a street car in Norfolk. The boy had been riding with two young men, who seemed to have been drinking.

"I spoke to him," said Pierce. "I said, 'Hello, Kenneth,' but he did not answer."

Norfolk—Harrison's older daughter, Anna Gallop, kept a boarding house there. Beasley went to Norfolk a few days later, talking to police and others. Again he heard nothing about his lost son.

Subsequent searches and inquiries were equally empty, for a full year and more. Hopefully, Samuel Beasley examined every hint, every rumor. With laudable calm and rationality, he refused to take legal action on mere hints and rumors. He continued to work his farm, to comfort as best he could his heartbroken wife, and to serve in the State Senate of North Carolina.

Eighteen months went by. The fall term of court for 1906 was begun at Currituck Courthouse. Beasley, attending the opening session in September, was hailed in the corridor by T. C. Woodhouse, brother of the storekeeper-postmaster. "I've got a message for you," he announced.

It was a message to which, we may be sure, Beasley listened with rapt interest.

On September 2, said Woodhouse, Joshua Harrison had met him in the road and had asked for "a heart to heart talk." Then, went on Woodhouse, Harrison had said: "Sam Beasley has never offered enough reward. When he does, the boy will show up in as good condition as he ever was." Further, said Woodhouse, Harrison had complained "it was damned expensive to keep the boy in the way he is being kept."

At once Beasley begged Woodhouse to return to Harrison and say that any amount of money would be paid for Kenneth's release, with no questions asked and no prosecution brought. Woodhouse departed, and a day later he sought out Beasley to report that Harrison had refused to discuss the matter, denying almost with tears his former remarks.

Also at the courthouse that September was A. B. Parker who, apparently at the urging of members of his family, offered some similar evidence. On the Saturday after Kenneth's disappearance, Parker told Beasley, Harrison had said in his hearing that "the boy wasn't lost; that he could put his hand on him any time he wanted him." All the months Parker had not mentioned this amazing statement because, as he now said, he felt that it was "none of his business."

This may seem to be discretion carried to a fantastic extreme; but there proved to be other Currituckans equally or more close-mouthed, enough of them to cause one to wonder if the habit of oppressive silence was not characteristic of the county in those times. J. L. Turner, who kept a store on the road above Poplar Branch, was only now prepared to say that, at the time of Kenneth's disappearance, he had seen Harrison driving a buggy with a dark mule in the shafts, and that in the buggy was a boy with his head covered by a tarpaulin or robe, but with brown-stockinged legs exposed.

Millard Morrisette was persuaded to tell of seeing the same mule-drawn buggy, with a man and boy riding in it, though he refused to say whether he recognized either. The boy, he said, wore a blue cap. Finally, W. E. Ansell, clerk of the superior court for Currituck, told substantially the same story. Ansell had seen the mule-drawn buggy along the road near his home in the northern part of the county. He had heard a child's voice complaining or pleading under the tarpaulin and had heard the driver speak reassuringly. The voice, Ansell was prepared to assure Beasley, was the voice of Joshua Harrison.

Beasley asked, and received, the promise of all these men to tell their stories in court. Then he swore out a warrant charging Harrison with kidnapping.

Placed under arrest, Harrison immediately denied the charge with considerable emphatic profanity. He hired distinguished counsel, including two ex-governors—his brother-in-law Thomas Jarvis and Charles B. Aycock—also E. F. Aydlett and I. M. Meekins. These asked for a change of venue, and the trial was accordingly set for the spring term of court in Pasquotank County. On March 14, in Elizabeth City, the case was called before Judge W. R. Allen.

Beasley had secured special prosecutors, J. Haywood Sawyer, W. M. Bond, and W. L. Cahoon. But the solicitor for the state, young Hallet S. Ward, had already begun to speak and act with the fiery potency that won him the nickname of "Hot Stuff" Ward, and never at any time did he show any timidity toward the brace of ex-governors who spoke for the defendant.

The trial lasted six days. Beasley was the first witness to appear for the prosecution. He told his story quietly and intelligently, though once or twice he spoke with a shaking voice, as though emotionally disturbed. He was followed by those who had talked to him at the Currituck Courthouse the previous September—the Woodhouse brothers, Turner the storekeeper, Parker, Ansell, Morrisette. Others corroborated the testimony of these men. Harrison sat glaring, his gray-bearded jaw set like granite.

Cross-examining witnesses, the defense lawyers elicited and clarified one fact to their case's advantage. The road in front of the Odd Fellows' Hall was an open one, lined with several houses to the west and facing the sound on the east. On the day of Kenneth's disappearance, the water had swarmed with fishing boats. Yet nobody could swear to a buggy, a dark-skinned mule, a gray-bearded driver. How, then, could Harrison have kidnapped Kenneth?

When it came the turn of the defense, evidence was offered that Harrison had been at home on the day in question, hard at work in his stable yard. All three of his sons swore to this. So did Mrs. Anna Harrison, whose manner on the stand was called frank and attractive. Rather less appealing was the appearance of her daughter and namesake, Mrs. Anna Gallop of Norfolk, who appeared to testify that Kenneth Beasley had never been brought to her lodging house.

"She was gaudily dressed, haughty in her bearing and simply full of unbecoming and unnatural display," writes one who was at the trial and whose sympathy was with the Beasleys. Another says that Mrs. Gallop was vigorously good looking, and that she successfully parried the efforts of the prosecutors to shake her story. At the end of her testimony, feeling a genuine triumph at what she felt was a successful appearance on her father's behalf, she fixed her eyes on Solicitor Ward.

"Now, sir," she said, "is there anything else you want to know about it? I have come a long ways to tell you, and I am ready to tell you whatever you want to know."

It might have embarrassed a man less ready of wit and

tongue than Hot Stuff Ward. But he smiled at her, with a fine show of gallantry.

"Only one thing, my dear madam, only one thing," he said gently. "Where is little Kenneth Beasley?"

Three neighbors supplemented the testimony of the Harrisons to the effect that the defendant had not left his farmyard from morning till night of February 13, 1905.

At the end of the presentation of defense evidence, the state offered several rebuttal witnesss. Two in particular— J. J. Woodhouse and D. F. Burfoot—testified that they were in Norfolk late on the night of February 13, and that they had both seen Joshua Harrison there.

Throughout the whole trial, attorneys for the two sides vied with each other in shrewdness of cross-examination. Efforts were made to impeach witnesses on charges of misconduct that ranged from chicken theft to betrayal of a "good working girl." On three separate occasions ladies were requested to leave the courtroom, perhaps to their disappointment, while such matters were discussed.

On March 19 the opposing counsel pleaded before the jury, and on the following day the judge delivered his charge and sent the jury to its room for deliberation. At ten o'clock that night, it returned to pronounce Joshua Harrison guilty of the charge of kidnapping.

Harrison bowed his head and wept. Several persons applauded, and Judge Allen hushed this demonstration with stern words. Governor Aycock, who was with his client, rose and in stirring terms asked that the verdict be set aside as prejudiced.

"The wail of a child in the night," he cried, "thrills and fills the hearts of men with such a passion that reason is blinded and someone must perhaps unjustly suffer. We fled from the passion of Currituck to get a fair trial here, and we find that Currituck has followed us and packed the court-room."

This was but an approach to Aycock's greater effort at courtroom drama. His voice dropped an octave as he faced the judge.

"Who," he inquired deeply, "will tell my loyal friend Jarvis of the jury's verdict and that his sister has perjured herself? The verdict has brought humiliation to the wife, disgrace to the children, and hopelessness to the grandchildren of Harrison. I want time in which the truth can be discovered, free from passion and prejudice. Women who are the pink of the city have broken into applause here—the feeling of the people broke into the jury box and influenced them. No action of Your Honor can take that influence out—come to the rescue of the law and set aside the verdict."

Solicitor Ward, too, was on his feet, and oratorical on his own part. He denied that he had charged Mrs. Harrison with perjury.

"Perjury catches its inspiration from a low, debased source," he said, "but loyalty and love that prompt a wife to swear for her husband, catches its inspiration from the heavens. When her statement was placed upon the Great Book above, the recording angel dropped a tear and blotted it out."

Judge Allen denied Governor Aycock's motion to set aside the verdict, then denied another motion for arrest of judgment.

"There are a number of questions concerning which I would have had some doubts," he said, "but those questions were for the jury to determine, and they found him guilty. The court is satisfied that the evidence was to them sufficient to convict him. The judgment of the court is that he be confined in the penitentiary at Raleigh for twenty years."

Harrison's lawyers appealed to the State Supreme Court for reversal of judgment. This appeal, which when published ran to thirty-six pages of print, brought forth once more the seemingly inexplicable fact that, if Harrison had kidnapped Kenneth Beasley, he must have done it under a cloak of invisibility—someone offshore or landward of the Sound Road would certainly have been him otherwise. Nor did it overlook the high feelings against the defendant. "When day after day the press of the State contained heart-rending accounts of the grief of the parents," the brief read in part, "and when at length it was stated in the press that suspicion was directed against the defendant, there arose not only in Currituck County but also in the State at large, a feeling of horror and indignation."

On September 17, the Supreme Court denied the appeal and ordered execution of judgment. On that day, Harrison sat alone in a room of the Gladstone Hotel in Norfolk. A city detective came into the lobby and sent a bellboy to ask Harrison so come down.

Harrison slammed the door in the boy's face. A moment later, the sound of a shot crashed out in the room. Bellboy and officer pushed in, and saw Harrison lying dead, a bullet hole in his temple and a pistol lying beside him. On a piece of hotel stationery he had written a last protest of his innocence.

At that same hour, Samuel Beasley was on his way to Arkansas, tracing a whisper that his boy was there, alive and waiting for him. Like so many other whispers, this led to nothing. Kenneth Beasley was never found.

Of those who recognized difficulties about the evidence

against Harrison, one of the most meditative in the years that followed was Solicitor Hallet S. Ward. His close friend and associate in the trial, W. M. Bond, often discussed the case with him. Bond, for many years a defense counsel of brilliant performance, felt strongly that the theory on which the state had contended that Harrison had carried off Kenneth was woefully weak.

Baffling, too, was the riddle of Joshua Harrison's state of mind. Those who had known him best were loth to believe that he was guilty. Quick-tempered and vengeful the man certainly was, but it seemed impossible that he would descend to so infamous a method of punishing his enemy Beasley. Too, there was his dying message, insisting on his innocence only moments before he took his own life. A lie is heavy freight to carry into the next world with one.

Twenty-seven years passed. Hallet Ward grew older, was twice elected to Congress, and, declining to seek a third term, returned to private practise. In 1934 he was motoring, with members of his family, to visit the site of the Lost Colony on Roanoke Island, and his way lay through Currituck County. At noon that day he turned at the village of Bertha to drive along State Highway 3 to the Sound. In front of the old hall where once Kennth Beasley had attended school the travellers spread their picnic lunch.

As they ate, two elderly farmers approached along the Sound Road. Ward, who makes friends easily, introduced himself.

"I have come here to look over the scene of my great lawsuit, the Harrison kidnapping," he told the two. "Were you gentlemen here at that time?"

"Yes," replied one, "and you never did get to the bottom of it."

As they talked, Ward mentioned the story about the recluse in the remote cabin. He remembered that the state had never been able to find this elusive fellow as a witness. His informants replied that the man had associated only with Harrison, buying wine from him, and kept a number of dogs.

At once Ward's mind flashed back to something he had heard of the last words Kenneth had ever spoken to his mother: "I've seen some mighty pretty puppies. . . ."

With his two new friends, he walked along a woods road, the same where Benny Walker had last seen Kenneth. Deep into the timber it went, and Ward could see an old rail fence with a rough stile. One of his companions pointed to a path on the other side of the fence. It led, said this man, to the house of the hermit.

A few more questions filled in details. A road came to the front of the cabin, from a northern stretch of the Sound Road well away from the Odd Fellows' Hall. Now, felt Ward, the old mystery was solved.

"Here," he said, "is the explanation of the case. Kenneth went up that path to that house so see those puppies. Harrison entered the gate in front of the house from the connecting road and picked the boy up at that house and drove on by the back road to the back gate and through it to the Sound Road and on to Norfolk."

As to the fate of the little fellow, Ward could imagine that. Harrison drove on to Norfolk with his prisoner. Kenneth's overcoat had been left behind—his father saw it a day later at the Odd Fellows' Hall. The night of February 13, 1905, was bitter cold, with a north wind blowing hard. Kenneth Beasley, not warmly dressed, contracted pneumonia, and died in some Norfolk hideaway.

"All my misgivings were relieved," confessed Ward after his pilgrimage to the scene of the kidnapping. But others along North Carolina's coast have persisted in the belief that Kenneth Beasley survived, grew to manhood and middle age, and is alive today under another name.

6

Poor 'Omi

"WHO PITIES THE ORPHAN?" wondered Braxton Craven, who was a Methodist minister, a college president, an author, and a philosopher and, to complete the catalogue, an orphan. "May the Lord pity him," hoped the Reverend Mr. Craven, "for man will not."

He spoke, despite the masculine pronoun, of a girl who had neither mother, father, nor luck. She was Naomi Wise— "poor 'Omi," they called her in Randolph County five generations ago and during generations more recent have so sung of her. She did win pity, but it was too late.

In the spring of 1808 she died, in a manner that has impelled some to think that Theodore Dreiser drew upon her plaintive history for his novel *An American Tragedy*. Dreiser himself said that his inspiration was a true story of upstate New York. However, the motive and method of Naomi Wise's slaying almost exactly resemble those set forth in Dreiser's novel, and, as shall be suggested in a later essay of this collection, possibly inspired imitation in something other than a written narrative. So romantic was the tale of Naomi Wise's fate that it was called fiction within recent years. However, study of the Randolph County court records, sketchy but plain, show that Naomi lived and, alas, untimely and violently died. There was a song about her, too, that has not wholly faded away.

Randolph County, lying close to North Carolina's heart, includes picturesque rocky heights and tree-bordered rushing streams, like illustrations in old-fashioned German novels. It was settled in the 1740's, partly by immigrants drifting down from Pennsylvania through Virginia and partly by westward-venturing pioneers from the coastal settlements. "There were developed," said the Asheboro *Evergreen* in 1851, "on the one hand, men who distinguished themselves for vice, rapine and the most villainous of crimes; on the other hand, men who displayed the noblest virtues and highest patriotism."

Randolphians were, and are, vigorous individualists. The classic hero of the county is Herman Husband, born and bred to the gentle Quaker faith, who nevertheless fought British Tories so bloodily well that King George's officers dispatched a special expedition to burn his house and lay waste his plantation. Similarly forgetful of Quaker tenets was Friend Jacob Cox. Riding home one day from market, he was accosted by three highwaymen, who told him to stand and deliver. From under his coat he whipped a most un-Quakerly pistol, and the robbers fled from before its levelled muzzle. For this exploit he was read out of meeting by the Society of Friends and was not readmitted until he had grown old and, it may have been felt, full of good will even toward highwaymen.

At the beginning of the nineteenth century, Randolph farmers of all godly denominations were celebrated for the quantity and quality of the brandy they distilled from their peaches. Randolph County brandy was a ready seller at the market in Fayetteville.

One of the Pennsylvanians to settle in Randolph County during colonial times was David Lewis. He had arrived, hint several commentators, a short, hurried jump ahead of the officers of that province's law. He built a cabin on Sandy Creek and fathered a number of sons—"tall, broad, muscular and very powerful men," says the account. They were handsome, too, quick of temper, and ready with gun, knife, or fist to a degree remarkable even among the roughest of the brandy-distillers and fur-trappers of the Deep River settlements. "They sought occasions of quarrel," adds the same historian, "as a Yankee does gold dust in California." It is not to be wondered at that very few Lewises died boresomely in bed.

Craven says that they scorned the law, but on occasion they would appeal to it. At the March term of court, in 1780, according to Randolph County's ancient minute book, the following judgment was recorded in favor of one of the family:

"That George Everby be recorded as a public liar, for speaking and propogating falsehood against Richard Lewis."

But Richard Lewis, whatever George Everby may have said against him, true or false, was able to take care of his own end of whatever violence came up.

Richard was a younger son of David, this lively family's founder. His brother Stephen, several years older than he, was so unthriftily hot-tempered as to shoot his horse, a very fine animal, when it fidgeted. Not long afterward his wife displeased him, and he flogged her with something called in those days a "hobble-rod." She fled from her home and spent several months so well hidden at a neighbor's house that her husband could not find her. Richard sought out Stephen, offering to persuade the runaway wife to return on promise of no more hobble-rod floggings. This promise Stephen gave, and Richard produced the lost lady.

She told her husband that it was Richard who had hidden her, and this struck Stephen as officious. He loaded his gun, announcing that he intended to shoot Richard on sight.

Thus determined, he approached Richard's home. Richard, seeing him in the yard and instantly certain of his purpose, seized his own gun and ran upstairs. Stephen came in at the front door, mounted the steps in turn, and was knocked back to their foot by a charge of shot.

Wounded but not cowed, he crept home. There he swore that as soon as he recovered he would go gunning for Richard again. Informed of this, the younger brother did not wait. He returned Stephen's fraternal call the same night. Peering through a space between the logs of the cabin wall, he saw Stephen sitting up in bed while someone bandaged his wounds. He aimed through the crack, and to better purpose than when threatened in his own home. His bullet struck Stephen in the heart.

He was exonerated on a plea of self-defense and moved across the line into Guilford County, where he built a house on Polecat Creek, near Centre Church. He had a son, Jonathan, who as he grew to manhood secured a job as clerk in the store of Benjamin Elliott in Asheboro. Jonathan boarded with his employer, but each Saturday night rode fifteen miles home, along the road that ran approximately where U.S. Highway 220 runs today. Each Sunday night he returned to Asheboro by the same route. His way took him past the home of William Adams in upper Randolph County.

Like all of the Lewis men, Jonathan was tall and strong,

and he was handsome as well. Braxton Craven called him "a large, well built, dignified looking man. He was young, daring and impetuous. . . . His smile like sunbeams bursting through a cloud, illumined every countenance upon which it fell." Such a figure, afoot or mounted on a good horse, would naturally attract a susceptible girl. As Jonathan Lewis passed the Adams farm weekend after weekend, he was glowingly watched by an orphan named Naomi Wise.

Naomi, with no parents or other relatives, had been bound out as a child to Mr. and Mrs. Adams, who, however, were fond of her and treated her with affection. She was nineteen years old in 1808. "Her size was medium," observed Braxton Craven, who heard about her from old neighbors, "her figure beautifully formed, her face handsome and expressive, her eyes keen yet mild, her words soft and winning." Other descriptions agree with this estimate, and it would appear that Naomi was industrious and cheerful as well as singularly pretty. She worked hard in the Adams kitchen, and on occasion wielded a hoe in the Adams fields. Mrs. Adams, a motherly soul, treated her as one of the family, dressing her well and lending her a horse to ride to church.

When Jonathan Lewis, riding to or from Asheboro, paused to ask her for a drink from the spring and then dismounted to carry her bucket to the house, she fell in love with him. As for Jonathan, he was considerably smitten on his own part. Again to quote Craven: "Her young and guiltless heart beat with new and higher life; that she was loved by a man so powerful as Lewis was sufficient recompense for a cheerless childhood." In the ordinary course of events, these two young people with Old Testament names would have married and lived happily ever after. Expecting to do just that, Naomi began to collect articles toward furnishing a home of her own—pots and pans, dishes, a chair, and a bed. Ever she watched for Jonathan's passing and welcomed him as he reined in and swung down from his saddle. In the dusk under the trees by the Adams' spring they spoke softly and held each other in close embrace, strong-built Jonathan and trim-built Naomi.

But Jonathan had a calculating mother, who knew that her son prospered in Benjamin Elliott's employment. She knew, too, that the Elliotts were high in reputation and bank balance, and that Benjamin Elliott had an unmarried sister named Hettie.

"That mothers are ambitious everybody knows," comments Braxton Craven sapiently, "and that they are the worst of matchmakers is equally well known." This is, however, philosophic epigram after the fact. Hettie Elliott would have been reckoned a good catch anywhere, though it is remembered that she was by no means as beautiful as Naomi Wise.

It was at his mother's insistence that Jonathan Lewis showed attention to Miss Elliott. She seemed not ill-pleased, and Elliott, the storekeeper, considered Lewis intelligent, industrious, and a respectable possibility as a brother-in-law. The courtship went forward on the almost routine pattern of those days—Lewis gallant and insistent, Miss Elliott encouraging but coy. Meanwhile, Lewis took to riding past the Adams farm without checking rein.

If he did not come there, the news of his attentions to Hettie Elliott did. Mrs. Adams lectured Naomi on the faithlessness of men in general, and of Jonathan Lewis in particular. Naomi wept, like many another jilted girl, and word of her weeping and its reason came back as far as Asheboro and the home of the Elliotts.

Hettie Elliott, who thus far had played the coquette, taxed

her suitor with the report that he was engaged to the pretty orphan girl who worked at the Adams farm.

"With coolness and steadiness which innocence is wont to wear," relates Craven, "Lewis affirmed to Miss Elliott that said rumor was a base, malicious slander, circulated by the enemies of the Lewis family to ruin his character, and offered that time, a very fair arbiter, should decide claim to her, Miss Elliott's hand."

If this indirect quotation is any earnest of Lewis' actual style of speech, it would seem that he was throwing his young life away clerking in Elliott's store. Such fiery periods sound like indications of a natural talent for Congress, even the Congress of 1808.

However worded, the disavowal of Naomi Wise impressed Miss Elliott favorably. Yet Lewis appeared uneasy during the days that followed, neglecting his business and seeming sick. After that, he began again to stop at the Adams place on his journeys between Asheboro and Polecat Creek, and Naomi continued to make him welcome, despite Mrs. Adams' advice.

On a spring afternoon—the exact day cannot be established—Naomi went out the kitchen door, pail in hand, as though to fetch water. She did not return for supper, or ever again.

Some miles southward along the road to Asheboro, an ancient ford spanned murmurous Deep River. Indians used it in centuries past, and later white traders headed across it for Fayetteville. Today a bridge crosses just north of Randleman where the old ford used to be. Above the ford, in 1808, John Hinshaw operated a grist mill, and directly beside the water stood the farm house of a widow named Mrs. Ann Davis. Darkness had settled down that evening, and Mrs. Davis sat with her two young sons beside the fire.

Suddenly, in the night outside, rose a loud, frantic scream, that abruptly throttled down into a gasping gurgle.

Up sprang Mrs. Davis, shrilling orders at her sons. They caught burning brands from the fireplace and ran out but could see nothing beyond the glare of their torches. As they made their way to the very brink of the river they heard loud splashing, then the sound of departing hoofs on the south side of the ford. The Davis boys peered and called to no avail. Finally they returned to the friendly lights of the house, unable to learn what had happened.

Meanwhile, at the Adams home, Naomi had been missed at supper and at bedtime. Mrs. Adams worried over her and slept badly that night. She rose before dawn, saying that she had been troubled by nightmares. She and her husband went out at the first gray light, and by the spring saw the empty pail Naomi had carried. Naomi's tracks led to a stump, and on the opposite side of that stump showed the marks of shod hoofs.

A horse, then, had come there, to stand while Naomi mounted behind the rider. William Adams sent to summon half a dozen other farmers, and the party followed the horse's trail away across fields. For several miles they traced the hoof marks to the Deep River ford.

The Davises were out, too, and hailed Adams with the story of that terrible scream in the night. Mrs. Davis' words, and something of her manner of speech, have been preserved in the account.

"Ah!" she said, "murder's been done, sich unyearthly screams can't come of nothing; they made the hair rise on my head, and the very blood curdle in my heart. O! ef I had been young as I once was, I would a run down there and killed the rascal afore he could a got away! What is the world a coming to?"

For all these stout protestations, neither Mrs. Davis nor her sons had yet explored for more evidence of what had befallen. With the coming of reenforcements, however, they made bold to search along the river. Very quickly it developed that Mrs. Davis' theory was correct. Murder had been done, of a certainty, and blood curdled in other hearts than hers.

A body lay half afloat among tangled weeds that grew on a muddy little bar near the shore. Several men waded in and dragged the body to firm ground. It was Naomi Wise, soaked, rumpled and dead.

Plainly her end had been a violent one. Her voluminous skirt had been pulled up around her face, as though to stifle those piteous screams. The white skin of Naomi's throat showed torn and bruised by powerful choking fingers. The coroner was fetched from Asheboro and empanelled a jury from among those gathered by the ford. "Drowned by violence," was the verdict they brought in. The coroner, making an examination added to this another fact—Naomi Wise had been expecting a child.

This intelligence caused faces to scowl, jaws to set. North Carolinians of that era took, concerning the seduction of trusting maidens, a view so dim as to be practically myopic. No more than sixteen years previously, something like a pattern toward such betrayals was set by young George L'Estrange of Wilmington. When his sister Matilda was seduced by James O'Neale, L'Estrange had waylaid that elegant spark and had discharged at him a huge horse pistol loaded with buckshot. Nine of these shot took effect in O'Neale's body, and he did not survive the day. O'Neale's subsequent death pleased doctors, ministers, and even officers of the law.

The sequel and the emotions it roused can best be described by Mason L. Weems, world-famous for his dissemination of the myth about Washington and the cherry tree:

"Many of the relatives of Mr. O'Neale, with all the libertines of the country, made great efforts to get young George L'Estrange condemned; but, to their immortal honor, the ladies of Wilmington and its vicinity, made still greater efforts for his safety and comfort. They spoke of him as their CHAMPION and AVENGER of their sex.

"His prison chamber was scoured and *furnished* as if for the reception of the great Washington. It was perfumed with odours and garnished with fairest flowers; and every day his board was spread with dainties, and every night his bed with down.

"In a little time the strength of the two parties was fairly tried in court; and the trembling YOUTH at the bar, with all his fair friends in the crowded galleries, heard the sentence of MANSLAUGHTER!

"Instantly the ladies dispatched a courier with a petition to Governor Martin for a *pardon,* which his excellency signed with great pleasure. The ladies then repaired to the prison and brought him forth in great triumph, and the next day escorted him to his father's house. . . ." *

In a word, he who killed a betrayer of trusting womanhood could fairly count on, not only immunity, but a flattering social success. The men beside Deep River expressed an immediate and earnest desire to track down Naomi's destroyer and to drink his blood. Who was he? Half a dozen voices

---

* *God's Revenge Against Adultery, Awfully Exampled In the Following Cases of American Crime.* Philadelphia, 1818. Capitals and italics are Weems's own.

offered the same name. Sheriff Isaac Lane deputized Robert Murdock to go looking for Jonathan Lewis.

Murdock did not find him that day at Elliott's store in Asheboro, nor yet at his home on Polecat Creek in Guilford County. However, Jonathan's matchmaking mother supplied Murdock with news, not guessing that it might damage her son. Jonathan had come home late the preceeding night, with wet clothes. He said that his horse had stumbled with him while crossing the river. Changing into dry things, he had ridden off again, presumably for Asheboro.

Back went Murdock, too, and learned more at the home of Colonel Joshua Craven. Mrs. Elizabeth Craven, the colonel's lady, said that Lewis had ridden up to her door in the early morning—at about the time, perhaps, that men were wading ashore with what they had fished from the water weeds at Deep River ford. Lewis' manner and expression had astonished the lady.

"What's the matter, Lewis, what have you been doing?" she had asked him. "Have you killed 'Omi Wise?"

It was a chance shot, but it had seemed to go home. Lewis had lifted his hand to his face. "Why, what makes you ask me that question?" he stammered.

"No particular reason," was Mrs. Cravens' answer, "only you look so pale and wild; you don't look at all like yourself this morning."

Lewis had then ridden away.

The deputy made more inquiries. The trail led him out of Asheboro, to the farm of a man named Hancock. An auction sale had been held there, and Murdock arrived late at night.

The sale had been something of a gala event, with refreshments and a dance, and Lewis had attended. Here, too, his manner had puzzled acquaintances as it had puzzled Mrs.

Craven. "During the day," says the narrative, "it was re-marked by many that Jonathan Lewis had a cast of counte-nance by no means usual. Instead of that bold, daring impudence that was usual to him, he seemed reserved, down-cast and restless. By indulging freely in drink, which was always to be had on such occasions, he became more like himself toward evening, and ventured to mingle with the ladies."

He showed special interest in Stephen Huzza's daughter Martha and, the Hancocks told Murdock, had left to escort Martha to her near-by home. Doggedly Murdock followed him to Huzza's.

The older people had gone to bed, and Jonathan sat in the parlor with Martha upon his lap. Murdock, accompanied by several friends, entered the house.

Encumbered by the young woman on his knee, Jonathan Lewis surrendered quietly. Murdock led him away—Martha Huzza must have stared blankly—and early the next morn-ing brought him to the Deep River ford, where Naomi Wise lay on a bier at the water side, surrounded by mourners.

Brought through the throng, Lewis stood looking down at Naomi's dead face silently. He put out his hand and smoothed her hair. This was taken by the onlookers as a sign of callous boldness; for, says Braxton Craven: "So greatly was the crowd incensed at this hard-hearted audacity, that the au-thority of the officer was scarcely sufficient to prevent the villain's being killed on the spot."

Naomi was buried beside the ford, and those who attended the funeral wept unashamedly. Jonathan Lewis was locked up in the jail at Asheboro. Craven calls it "the strong jail, that then towered in Asheboro as a terror to evil doers." Less enthusiastically, the minute book of the Randolph County court for 1808 says that the building was of "shackley frame."

Stubbornly the prisoner protested his innocence, with few to listen and fewer to believe. The evidence against him was circumstantial but awkward. It seems to have included several interesting exhibits: "The footprints from the stump to the river exactly fitted his horse; hairs upon the skirt upon which [Naomi] rode, were found to fit in color; a small piece torn from Lewis' accouterment, fitted both rent and texture; his absence from Asheboro, and many other circumstances all conspired to the same point."

He was the only prisoner confined on a murder charge at that time, and outside his barred window gathered throngs of citizens. Some of these spoke insistently of taking him out of jail and hanging him in the public square, sparing the state the troublesome formality and expense of a trial and giving a wholesome example of what might be expected by those who violently eliminate unwanted sweethearts. So threatening did this sort of conversation become that the county officials appointed Benjamin Elliott, Lewis's erstwhile employer, captain of a guard of twelve men. These took turns at standing armed watch over the jail for full thirty days. Their names are still preserved in the minute book.

The situation must have convinced Lewis that he had little to hope for if brought to trial. At the end of the thirty days he managed to escape from jail, perhaps with the aid of relatives. This time there was no tracing of his tracks as he fled.

Meanwhile, a song had begun to be heard in Randolph County. It began in the familiar come-all-ye fashion that characterizes many Old World folk rhymes:

Come all you good people, I'd have you draw near,
A sorrowful story you quickly shall hear;

A story I'll tell you about 'Omi Wise,
How she was deluded by Lewis' lies.

In the second stanza, the narration shifted to first person, as though Naomi herself sang from her unmarked grave by Deep River:

He promised to marry and use me quite well,
But conduct contrary I sadly must tell,
He promised to meet me at Adams' Springs,
He promised me marriage and many fine things.

These lines are stilted, not to say repetitious. They do not read with the savory vigor of a couple of other songs later to be quoted in this work. Yet the spirit and purport of the verses, and those that followed, were heard with no relish by Jonathan Lewis's kinsmen. Worst of all was the last of them:

The wretch then did choke her, as we understand,
And threw her in the river, below the mill dam.
Be it murder or treason, Oh! what a great crime
To murder poor 'Omi and leave her behind.

The Lewises began to depart, family by family, from a county that sang so reproachfully of their family name. Years passed, and report drifted back that they had settled in Kentucky, just south of the Ohio River. By 1814, six years after Naomi's tragic death and Jonathan Lewis's escape and flight, Jonathan himself was said to be living in the new Lewis settlement, married and the father of a son.

Memory of the tragedy had been kept specially green by the song. When news came of Lewis's whereabouts, the whole community urged his capture. "Justice cried, 'Cut the sinner down,'" wrote Craven. "Indignation cried, 'Shame to the lingering servants of law.'"

The lingering servants of law in Randolph County were such as hearkened dutifully to the popular wish of voters and taxpayers. The county trustees met and voted to go after Lewis. Isaac Lane chose Colonel Craven and sturdy young George Swearengain as his partners on the adventure.

This trio reached the neighborhood of the Lewis settlement, and learned of Jonathan Lewis's presence there. Then they paused to take council. All three were known to him, and their appearance would put him and his relatives on guard. Finally they engaged two hunters, for $75, to capture their man for them.

This pair of amateur catchpolls followed Lewis to a house where a dance was in progress. The dialogue between them and the host, as repeated by Craven, is backwoodsy enough to furnish a novel by Mayne Reid:

"Hallo, to the man of the house and all of his friends."

"Hallo back to you, and maybe you'd light and look at your saddle."

"Apt as not, if we're allowed to see our saddles on the peg, our hosses eatin' fodder, and ourselves merry over hog and hominy."

"Ef you are what you look like, and not Yankee speculators, or bamboozled officers, nor Natchez sharpers, you are welcome to sich as we have."

"And s'pose we are not what we look like, what then?"

"Why, the sooner you move your washing the better; we're plain, honest folks here and deal with scatterlopers arter their deserts."

"Well, well, we'll light and take some of your pone and a

little of your blink-eye, and maybe as how we'll get better acquainted."

After this pert exchange, the two hunters were admitted to the house and took part in the merry-making. They saw Jonathan Lewis, dressed in fringed buckskin, with a hunting knife at his belt. There was another picturesque conversation, Lewis speaking first:

"I reckon you are strangers in these parts."

"I reckon we are, being we know nobody and nobody knows us; and we are perlite enough not to trouble strangers with foolish questions, and so I guess we shall still be strangers."

"But maybe we all came from the same land, and so might scrape an acquaintance easier than you think."

"As to that, it's no difference, without telling or asking names, we give the right hand to every honest hunter."

"Then you're hunters I s'pose, and as we have a great deer hunt tomorrow, perhaps you'll join."

"That we will, ef it's agreeable."

The pair attended the hunt as invited and stayed close to Lewis. As he drew away from the others, they leaped upon him, overpowered him and tied his hands securely. They then marched him to where Sheriff Lane and his companions lay hidden.

Paying the two hunters who had scored so well at repartee and man-catching, Lane's party started quickly for North Carolina with its prisoner. They made several forced marches to get beyond any threat of pursuit by members of the violent Lewis family. Then one night, as they paused to make camp, Lewis slipped his bonds and ran.

He was swift of foot and quickly distanced Lane and Craven. Swearengain, young and athletic, achieved a burst of speed, overtook Lewis and tackled him like a footballer. As the two struggled on the ground, the others came panting up and helped make Lewis fast as before.

Back in the Randolph County jail, Lewis was unable to escape again from its shackley confines. He pleaded for a trial in a county less prejudiced against him than Randolph. The court granted him a change of venue to Guilford where, early in 1815, the trial began.

Witnesses included Mrs. Mary Adams, Naomi's motherly guardian; Benjamin Elliott, who had employed Jonathan Lewis and later had guarded him in his cell; Hettie Elliott Ramseur, now married to someone else and extremely glad of it; Elizabeth Craven, who had seen Lewis flinch when asked if he had killed Naomi Wise; Ann Davis, who had heard the scream in the night; Robert Murdock, who had arrested Lewis in Huzza's parlor.

Their testimony was not enough. Somehow—it would be interesting to know exactly how—Lewis managed to convince judge and jury of his innocence. Whatever his methods, they did not depend on a long purse, for the minute book of Randolph County's court for the February term of 1815 carries the following notation, curiously phrased but understandable:

"Ordered of the Court that the County Trustees pay the cost and charges of attorneys. The prosecution of Jonathan Lewis for felony when trial is removed to the County of Guilford to the said Jonathan Lewis there requested and said discharged from jail under the ensolvent [sic] Debtors Act."

Thus free in Guilford County, he headed swiftly westward for Kentucky, sensibly avoiding any farewell visit to Randolph.

He did not live long. Sickness overcame him in about 1820,

and the story trickled back to Asheboro that he had died confessing his guilt.

Apparently his admission was a long and circumstantial one. Poor Naomi had begged him tearfully to marry her. When he neglected her, she hinted prosecution for breach of promise. Jonathan's suit for the hand of Hettie Elliott had been much endangered by Naomi's complaints, audible all the way to Asheboro. Therefore Jonathan had met his former sweetheart a last time by Adams' spring, saying that he had come to take her to a preacher and marry her.

Brushing aside her suggestion that they be married at the Adams home, he induced her to mount behind his saddle and rode with her to the ford, where he told her that he was determined to kill her. Frantically she begged for her life, then screamed in terror. Muffling her cries in her skirt, Jonathan strangled her to death and threw her body into the river. Then he rode across to the other side as torches appeared at the door of the Davis home.

"He declared," Braxton Cravens' narrative ends, "that while in prison Naomi was ever before him; his sleep was broken by her cries for mercy, and in the dim twilight her shadowy form was ever before him, holding up her imploring hands. Thus ended the career of Jonathan Lewis, for no sooner was his confession completed than his soul seemed to hasten away."

Braxton Craven wrote his story perhaps as early as 1840, drawing upon the first-hand accounts of those who had known both Naomi and her false lover. In later years he discouraged proposals to publish this effort, referring to it as a "schoolboy composition, crude and unpolished." Finally he relented, and in 1874 it appeared under the pen name of Charlie Vernon, in the columns of the Greensboro *Patriot*.

Later it was brought out as a paper-backed pamphlet and was republished as recently as 1944.

Naomi had other memorials. In 1879, when J. E. Walker, John H. Ferree, J. O. Pickard, and Amos Gregson established a cotton mill at the old ford of Deep River, they named it Naomi Factory. Around the site grew up the thriving town of Randleman. The name of the murdered girl was further preserved in Naomi Falls and the Naomi Methodist Church. Nor has the name of Naomi been uncommon among Randolph County girls. The river still croons sadly, as though chanting the old, pathetic song.

The song itself was echoed beyond Randolph County for many years. Probably it was well known in the mountains of Burke County in the late 1860's, by a banjo-picker named Tom Dula. That story is coming.

7

A Bullet for Nimrod

POSSIBLY THE RESIDENTS of Macon County are right in claiming for their home region the utmost in wild beauty throughout the North Carolina mountains. Macon is a high county. Some forty-seven of its peaks have altitudes of more than 4,000 feet, and the lowest dip toward sea level is 1,900 feet, at the point where the Little Tennessee River flows across the line into Swain County. Two picturesque and fertile river valleys, the Little Tennessee and the Nantahala, run through Macon, and they are sentinelled in every direction by mountains with intriguing names—Standing Indian and Wine Spring Bald, Fodderstack and Lamb and Burningtown and Pinnacle, Scaly and Fish-hawk and Pickens' Nose, Wildcat Cliff and Cartoogeehaye and Bear Pen. Franklin, the county seat, was built upon the site of the Sacred Town of the Cherokees and therefore may be, by inheritance at least, the oldest settlement in the state.

And some of Macon's citizens have been as rugged as Macon's topography. Around 1820 the first white settlers trickled in, as soon as the land had been purchased from the

Cherokee Indians. Records on those first settlers are scant but, so far as they go, illuminating.

They were farmers then, as most of them are farmers now. In clearing, sowing, and cultivating acres of mountainside soil, in building cabins and fences, the pioneers of Macon County early established a custom of mutual help. Thus, neighbors made up harvesting crews, to reap and shock crop after crop in order of ripening. To carve a field out of the forest, to build a home of logs, or to maul out a thousand or two rails for his fence, a man need only to call for help upon surrounding homesteads, and the labor would be completed in a day. He would be ready, of course, to help in his turn any and all others of his neighborhood.

Another Macon County custom, more picturesque and more specialized to the region, was that of the semi-formal fistic duel. As gentlemen in broadcloth, down in the lowlands, settled differences with pistols, so the mountain men settled theirs with knuckles. The Reverend C. D. Smith wrote, in 1891, *A Brief History of Macon County, North Carolina,* and he harked back to the stirring scenes of his youth with a zest that whispers of muscular Christianity.

"When these contests took place," he remembered, "the custom was for the parties to go into the ring. The crowd of spectators demanded fairness and honor. If any one was disposed to show *foul play* he was witheld or in the attempt promptly chastised by some bystander. Then again, if either party in the fight resorted to any other weapon than his physical appendages, he was at once *branded and denounced as a coward,* and was avoided by his former associates."

The italics here are the reverend doctor's own and give good evidence of his enthusiastic and not impractical notions about how to wage a skull-and-knuckle fight. This wager of battle tradition was so earnestly upheld in Macon County that when, some time in the late 1820's, a Tennessee bully named Keen spoke loudly and boastfully in the streets of Franklin, it was no less a Maconian than Edward Poindexter who challenged him.

Poindexter was a justice of the peace, an influential figure in the county's organization, and a man of property and family. He was also handy with his fists; Esquire Poindexter so beat and mauled his opponent that, remembered Dr. Smith, "the Tennesseean went away the next day bruised and sore with his game feathers drooping all around him."

This description of early scuffles is prefatory, in Dr. Smith's work, to notice of what by 1891 had been a different and more baleful usage for a couple of decades—the carrying of pistols.

"It is, dear reader," sets forth our man of God, "an open question as to whether Colt, Wesson and others with their patented inventions and manufacture of pistols have not been the greatest national scourge of the age. With the pistol has come an avalanche—an inundation of robberies. They bear the ear-marks of pistol paternity. It is the revolver that arrests the railway train, goes through the express and mail cars, appropriating their contents, and rifles the pockets of innocent passengers without regard to age, sex or condition. It is the chief reliance of the assassin. It steals into the apartments of decrepitude and old age at the still hour of midnight and leaves them stripped of their valuables and occupied by death."

As Dr. Smith committed these words to paper, he could not but have remembered with sadness his old friend, Colonel Nimrod S. Jarrett of Apple Tree Farm, who had died of a pistol bullet just nineteen years before.

Nimrod Jarrett had a dynamic vigor of body and character

that made him a fitting namesake for the mighty hunter before the Lord who is credited, in the Book of Genesis, with founding the fearsome empire of Assyria.

His grandparents came from Pennsylvania in colonial times, and settled in Buncombe County, where Jarretts have flourished ever since. Young Nimrod, born in 1800, was a good farmer and hunter from his boyhood upward but lacked money to buy land of his own. His chance came when a doctor named Hailen arrived from Philadelphia, to establish on Jonathan's Creek near the Jarrett home a factory for drying and shipping ginseng root.

Ginseng is, of course, the root used from antiquity among the Chinese as a restorer of masculine potency. Most modern scientists agree that its effect is merely a psychic one, but through the centuries it was used so extensively in China that it became scarce and almost prohibitively costly. The Imperial Government declared its gathering unlawful, and ginseng poachers were liable to an official shortening by the height of a head. American ginseng, that grows naturally in the Appalachians, then became an item of lively trade with the Chinese.

Nimrod Jarrett began to prowl the Buncombe County groves to find ginseng for Dr. Hailen. The doctor paid seven cents a pound for the green root, and the young man, then twenty years old, contrived to fetch in such quantities at that figure as to be able to save money. Save money he did, during ten years of ginseng hunting, and by 1830 he was well enough supplied to buy a farm in Haywood County. Meanwhile he had married the daughter of James McKee, who lived on Jonathan's Creek near Dr. Hailen's ginseng factory.

In Haywood County, Jarrett raised corn and between whiles continued to gather ginseng and to sell it to Dr. Hailen.

By 1835 he was ready to move again, this time to Franklin County, where he bought large tracts of land.

He was industrious, capable, and lucky. He built houses at Franklin and Aquone, both of which communities grew so as to enhance the value of his property. In Swain County he bought more land, which proved to contain talc deposits, minable at a gratifying figure. The Macon County militia, an enthusiastic military establishment that included in its ranks practically every able-bodied male, was his special interest. He served as captain, then as colonel. In 1850 and afterward he bore his important part in the militia's ambitious program of laying out and building various county roads.

His home he made at Aquone—"The sound of waters" is the meaning of that beautiful Cherokee name—until, in 1855, tragedy swooped down. The house blazed with mysterious fire in the night. All the occupants managed to scramble clear except Jarrett's youngest daughter, who was trapped in a bedroom and perished miserably. Mrs. Jarrett, trying frantically to rescue the girl, had been held back forcibly from plunging into the flames.

From the sadness that now shrouded Aquone, Jarrett moved and built himself a comfortable house in the Nantahala Valley six miles to the northward. He named his new home Apple Tree Farm, for the orchard he planted. His name went on the land in that district, and it can be heard today— Jarrett's Ford, Jarrett's Knob, Jarrett's Station. He was living there in 1872, and in the early dawn of September 15 of that year he and Mrs. Jarrett rose, ate breakfast, and made ready to travel.

Colonel Nimrod S. Jarrett, as old as the century, yet remained active and healthy. He proposed to ride some twenty miles to Franklin that day, for the transaction of real estate business.

That would be a long ride, up slope and down, and perhaps he bustled about his preparations. Mrs. Jarrett, though some years younger than he, moved more slowly and painfully by reason of an attack of crippling rheumatism. At last she bade her husband saddle up and ride ahead. After all, she intended to accompany him no farther than Aquone, where she planned to stay with their daughter, Mrs. Addie Jarrett Munday, until Nimrod's return from Franklin. Nimrod might leave first, but he would naturally keep his horse to a walk, saving its strength for the long trip through Wayah Gap to the county seat. His wife, with a shorter journey, could follow later at a brisker pace and catch up with him.

This advice made the best of sense to Nimrod Jarrett, and he mounted his horse and set out alone.

The first part of his journey lay through a magnificient stretch of gorge along the Nantahala. On one side flowed the swift water, on the other rose steep slopes, grown thick with trees. Doubtless the leaves showed forth autumn's earliest promise of the rioting wealth of color to come. Nimrod Jarrett saw, on the trail ahead of him, a trudger on foot. He overtook this man, spoke to him in friendly greeting, and then passed ahead, and so into eternity.

Back at Apple Tree Farm, Mrs. Jarrett mounted her own horse and set out, half an hour or so behind her husband, intent on finding him quickly.

She found him at a point where the trail wound through tangled riverside thickets. There he lay face down, limp and motionless. He did not stir or speak when she called to him. Leaning from her saddle, Mrs. Jarrett saw the unexampled brightness of red blood on his shirt collar, flowing from a wound where the back of his neck met his skull.

At such a discovery as that, almost any woman would scramble down from her horse and dissolve into helpless lamentations. Not so Mrs. Jarrett, so suddenly aware that she was a widow. Her forbears had marched in buckskin to the battle of King's Mountain, and now she revealed bravery and presence of mind worthy of such descent. Shaking her bridle, she rode past and away from her dead husband, and made all the haste she could to the house of Micajah Lunsford, half a mile beyond.

This mountain farmer was every bit as individual and sturdy as his name sounds. He came to his door at Mrs. Jarrett's loud call, and apparently he listened with unstampeded interest to what she told him. Then he suggested that she ride on to summon others from the houses next to his. He himself snatched a rifle and hurried on foot to the spot where Jarrett lay.

When his neighbors began to gather, they found Lunsford standing guard over the body. In a short time, little more than an hour, at least a score of people had gathered, and in attitude and behavior showed themselves intelligently practical.

These were all mountain men, bred to skill in hunting and stalking, and withal sternly in favor of justice upon criminals. "Short work with a long rope," says the old formula of the Smokies for dealing with murderers. Meanwhile, as in another quaint aphorism, the celebrated recipe for jugged hare, the quarry must first be caught. There on the brink of the Nantahala, nobody was so clumsily thoughtless as to press close to where Nimrod Jarrett lay on his dead face—not until

Micajah Lunsford and one or two others of tried trailing experience moved carefully in and squatted down to look.

The most sapient of professional detectives would have approved of their sober discussion. Plainly Jarrett had been shot from behind, and had fallen to die instantly, while his startled horse had gone trotting away. Might the killer have taken the horse? Nobody could rightly say at the moment; but meanwhile, here were tracks beside Jarrett's body, deep and plain, where someone had stood and stooped. See, volunteered an observer, how the toes sank into the soft earth. The man who had shot Jarrett had then come close to plunder his victim's pockets.

Several pairs of woods-wise eyes studied those tracks. One of the group picked up a stick, and with its help began to make careful measurements.

In the cluster with Lunsford around the body were such men as Z. D. Winters, A. J. Shields, Jefferson Martin, Jacob Franklin, and Thomas Wilson. It cannot be established which of the various clues can be credited to which man's finding or rationalization; quite probably there was considerable grave discussion and a mutual building, just as these same men might work together at a house-raising or rail-mauling. Others whose names do not survive stood at a greater distance to watch, taking care to obscure no tracks or other marks. Into this outer circle now drifted a shabby newcomer by the name of Balis Henderson.

He was young and completely undistinguished in appearance, and Lunsford and some of the others knew him slightly. Only recently he had made his appearance in the district, saying that he had come from Tennessee. One memorialist calls him a tramp, another a desperado. Likely he deserved neither of these designations, for he had been looking, none too steadfastly to be sure, for farm work, and had said that he wanted to settle down. Just now his legs and feet were wet. This must have drawn the attention of one of the group to them.

"Your shoes are just the size of those tracks," said this observant Maconian, pointing.

Henderson appeared irritated and came to look.

"I never made those tracks," he protested, and added that he had just then waded across a shallow place in the river, to see what had caused the crowd to gather. Then he lifted a foot. "I do not have heels on my shoes," he said.

No more he had. But then another man of the circle said harshly that the shoes looked as if the heels had been knocked off very recently, perhaps only a few minutes ago. Another fellow was tracing the foot-marks from beside Jarrett's body and called out that they led into the river. All right, maybe Balis Henderson had waded twice across the Nantahala at this point.

The Tennesseean began to goggle, to whine, to shake in his wet heelless shoes. Two tall men came up on either side of him and seized his elbows.

"You are under arrest," said one of them in his ear.

A search of Henderson's pockets brought to light a single-barreled pistol. Its value, as a subsequent court document informs us, was two dollars. Somebody sniffed the muzzle—the weapon had been fired recently. Next, Henderson's shoes were stripped from his soggy feet and compared narrowly with the tracks beside the body. They matched exactly, save for the missing heels.

Among the onlookers there were not wanting those to suggest that Henderson be hanged immediately to any of the trees that abounded so conveniently around the scene of

Jarrett's murder. More sober opinion prevailed. Several volunteers procured horses, and that very day Balis Henderson was escorted to Franklin, where Sheriff James Candler locked him up in jail.

On the following day, September 16, Judge Riley H. Cannon convened a grand jury, which made short work of indicting Henderson for the crime of murder in the first degree. His trial was set for the December term of court at Franklin.

Despite the laudable forbearance observed by those who in the Nantahala Gorge had regarded the dead Jarrett and the living Henderson, Macon County buzzed with eagerness to see the accused man hanged. Nobody seemed to doubt his guilt, however frantically he denied it, and for a time no lawyer at the county seat felt prepared to take his case.

At last he procured an attorney, William L. Norwood. This young man, who in his teens taught a country school, had gone to Arkansas in 1861 and there, at the age of twenty, had enlisted in the Confederate Army to serve throughout the Civil War. An old story, without any surviving published or written authority that can be traced, says that he was sympathetic to Henderson because they had soldiered together. Norwood engaged an associate for the defense, Kope Elias, and they moved at once for change of venue on the reasonable ground that no impartial jury could be empanelled for Henderson in Macon County. Their request was granted, and at Webster, then county seat of Jackson County, the trial began on December 18.

The presiding judge was James L. Henry, whose life was a succession of precocities. He was born in Buncombe County in 1838, of a seventy-three-year-old father who had fought in the Revolutionary War at the age of fourteen but who followed the profession of law until he died, at a hale ninety-seven. James Henry received a rather casual education in the common schools of Asheville, but before he was ten years old had acquired the habit of reading classics in several languages. At nineteen he became editor of the Asheville *Spectator,* succeeding in that post the incomparably picturesque Zebulon Vance. In his spare time Henry read law, but in 1861 gave up both journalism and study to join the hard-riding First North Carolina Cavalry. This has been called the best mounted unit in the Army of Northern Virginia, and Henry left it to be a colonel at the age of twenty-six. From the war he returned to gain admission to the bar, and after acting as solicitor of the Eighth Judicial District, he was elected a judge of Superior Court when he was thirty. When he died at forty-eight, he was described as having lived and succeeded enough for four centenarians.

Henderson's trial lasted but a single day, and Norwood and Elias could offer but little solid defense against the overwhelming circumstantial evidence presented in the testimony of such witnesses as Micajah Lunsford and his fellow mountaineers. The heelless shoes, and the bullet from Jarrett's skull that matched the pistol from Henderson's pocket, made telling exhibits for the prosecution. The jury spent but a short time in agreeing that Henderson was guilty as charged.

When the verdict was announced, Norwood rose to ask that it be set aside. The indictment for murder, he pointed out, accused Henderson of killing "one N. S. Jarrett," whereas the evidence had been to the effect that the dead man was named Nimrod S. Jarrett.

Judge Henry overruled the motion, and Norwood sat down again. Then it was that, in some way not fully remembered today, a difference of opinion broke out between Henderson and his attorneys.

Some light is cast upon this by what Henderson himself ventured to tell the judge, asking for a new trial. "I have discovered evidence," he said in part, "that would have been material and important to me . . . and my counsel did not advise me of its materiality."

If these are Henderson's actual words, they go far toward absolving him of that slurring designation of "tramp." He must have been able to speak articulately and even in legal phraseology. However, he would not elaborate upon the nature of this new evidence, and Judge Henry felt obliged to deny this plea as well. He pronounced upon Henderson the sentence of death by hanging and sent him back to jail.

The convicted murderer was now without a lawyer, Norwood and Elias having withdrawn from the defense following the dispute. From his cell Henderson wrote, again with evidence of education and ability to handle language, an appeal that the State Supreme Court review his case. He said that he was a very poor man and without funds to pay the necessary court costs, but he begged the justices to be generous and give him consideration.

Consideration he received. Again Henderson said nothing about new evidence, but raised the question about the difference between the names of N. S. Jarrett and Nimrod S. Jarrett. Justice Thomas Settle, writing an opinion for his colleagues, met this disingenuity with a grave dissent.

"The name is generally required as the best mode of describing the person," he said weightily, "but he may be described otherwise, by his calling or the like, if he be identified thereby, as the individual and distinguished from all others. . . . It would appear to be a nice refinement to arrest a judgment for an informality in setting forth the name of the person injured, since it is a common practice with most persons to write their christian names sometimes in full and sometimes by the initials only."

Justice Settle summed up by saying that the Supreme Court concurred unanimously in upholding the verdict of the jury and the sentence of the judge of the Superior Court in Jackson County.

It may be wondered what hopes poor Balis Henderson had entertained of rescue when he offered so poorly founded an appeal. Whatever they were, they now left him and were replaced by desperation. He contrived to escape from the jail at Webster, at a moment when guards were absent. Sheriff William Bumgarner deputized a posse of men from Jackson and Macon counties to bring him back.

Again North Carolina mountain men discomfited Henderson by their skill in tracking. They decided that he would try to head home for Tennessee and accordingly set their search in that direction. He was traced to a heap of brush, in which he had sheltered like a hunted rabbit. They dragged him out and back to the jail at Webster.

This broke his spirit. A few days later he made a full confession of the murder.

True enough, he now admitted, he had killed Colonel Nimrod Jarrett. He had known, many of the neighbors had known, that Jarrett would be carrying a considerable sum of money with him on his visit to Franklin. Wherefore, Henderson had contrived to be walking along the Nantahala River trail, loaded pistol in pocket, on the same morning that Jarrett would come riding past. He had returned Jarrett's friendly salutation and had walked a short distance beside the horse. Then he had fallen back a pace, drawn his pistol and shot Jarrett in the back of the neck.

He hurried to search Jarrett's pockets, taking a gold watch, but finding only a few coins. Possibly the bulk of the money Jarrett had brought was in his saddle bags, and the horse had fled. Then Henderson heard the sound of more hoofs approaching and had splashed across the river to hide. The new rider was Mrs. Jarrett, and shortly she had summoned neighbors to the scene. Henderson had hidden Jarrett's watch and chain in a hollow tree—let someone go look, he said, and a man named Holland was sent. Holland brought back the watch and chain and a handful of money.

In May of 1873, the officials of Jackson County caused to be built a rough but serviceable scaffold at Webster, and upon it they hanged Balis Henderson by the neck until he was dead.

One more mystery remained unsolved for a full quarter of a century beyond. Then, in 1898, a scoundrelly old man named Bill Dills lay dying in his ramshackle cabin on Wusser Creek.

Weakly, gaspingly, he said that he, like Henderson, had a confession to make. Back in 1855, he had prowled the home of Nimrod Jarrett at Aquone, had taken a sum of money, and then had set the house afire to cover his crime. That was how Jarrett's little daughter had died.

So saying, Bill Dills died, too, and folks reckoned that he went from there to shake hands with Balis Henderson, down somewhere in the root cellar of hell where it is supposed to be hotter than ever that fire had flamed at Aquone.

Dr. Smith, the Macon County historian, might have wished to give these two the company in inferno of Messrs. Colt and Wesson.

"Now cast up in your mind," he finished his essay, "the immense destruction of human life in which the pistol has been the most potent instrument—the woes and anguish that have settled down upon the innocent and helpless on its account—the sad weeds of widowhood and orphanage, with which the once happy domestic altar has been shrouded ... and tell me what this *infant industry* has done for the nation. It seems to me that a little prohibition along this line might do the nation some good."

8

The Life and Death of Chicken Stephens

BY THE SPRING OF 1870, State Senator John Walter Stephens of Caswell County—"Chicken" Stephens, he was euphemistically called—had thriven in the arts of swindling, terrorism, and ballot-box stuffing to a height of accomplishment and renown that excited the envious admiration of all the political pirates who administered North Carolina's graceless Reconstruction government.

Like many another person destined for success and advancement, he had won his position without influence of family or background. He was born in 1834, near Bruce's Crossroads in Guilford County, and back of him stretched a line of forbears unromantically industrious and honest. His father, Absalom, was a respected tailor, and his mother, Letitia, was a gentle, worn housewife of earnest but not truculent Christian faith. Shortly after John's birth, the Stephens family moved to Rockingham County and settled in Leaksville. The tailor died in about 1840, poor but sincerely mourned by his family and friends. To his children he left, wrote an acquaintance, "the invaluable legacy of a good name." Little else in his estate could comfort them, and his fellows of the Masonic Lodge of Leaksville built a home for the widow and orphans.

John Stephens grew to be tall and slender, with light hair, blue eyes, and a fair complexion. His disposition was called "amiable," and his talent was for the easy amassing of money. He became a harness-maker and managed while still new to the trade to cheat a decent old tanner out of leather valued at $75. He likewise victimized one Hugh Wheeley in a horse trade, by snatching away a note for payment of "boot" and riding off with it. These adventures were not so notorious as to prevent his holding minor office in the Methodist Church at Wentworth, the county seat, or becoming agent for the American Bible and Tract Society for the counties of Rockingham and Caldwell. He married Miss Nancy Waters, and then moved to South Carolina to engage in tobacco buying. Along with a few other of South Carolina's male citizens in 1861, he had no enthusiasm for joining the army of the new Confederacy and hired a substitute to go in his stead.

Within a year or so he returned to Rockingham County. For a while he served as an impressment agent for the Confederate government. Then came indications that he himself would be impressed, as part of Dixie's final effort to oppose the advance of William Tecumseh Sherman, but he ran into legal difficulties that kept him out of gray uniform.

His neighbor, Thomas A. Ratliff, missed two chickens and found their headless carcasses in Stephens' hands. Arrest on a charge of larceny followed. Stephens gave bail of $500 in Confederate money and at once went to find Ratliff, armed with a club and a pistol. He attacked his accuser on the streets of Wentworth. Several bystanders tried to separate them and were wounded by Stephens' pistol bullets, but Ratliff was unhurt. Again under arrest, Stephens made bail of $2,000 and at the next term of court paid fines both for the theft of the chickens and the assault.

That was February of 1865. Within two months, a war had ended in withering defeat, and a peace that was no peace had begun.

Lee's army had been paroled at Appomattox, and Johnston's at Greensboro. Lincoln's plans for a sane restoration of the Union, with malice toward none and with charity for all, went suddenly to the grave with him, and his policies concerning malice and charity were exactly reversed throughout the conquered South. Leaders of the lost Confederacy found themselves proscribed. W. W. Holden, once a Unionist, then a secessionist, changed coats and sides once more and got himself named as governor by the victors at Washington. Reconstruction came upon North Carolina like all ten of Egypt's plagues at once.

Stephens now made ready to move to Yanceyville, county seat of Caswell County, where once he had sold Bibles. Before doing that, however, he quarrelled frighteningly with his sister, so that she fled to the home of a neighbor. Stephens made capital of this occurrence, arranging that his mother follow her daughter on a visit. He then sold the house given his mother by the Masons, pocketed the money, and moved his wife and two small daughters to Yanceyville.

There, as in Rockingham County, he attended the Methodist church. Very soon, his fellows in that congregation felt pained to see that Stephens was consorting with the more unsavory of the local Reconstructionists. Dr. Allen Gunn made it his business to protest to Stevens against such association.

Stephens replied that his object was to make money. In pursuit of that object, he offered to deliver to Dr. Gunn the vote of the entire county for sheriff if the doctor would pay him, Stephens, the sum of $4,000.

"I would not bribe any man at the price of one cent," said Dr. Gunn angrily.

"You are behind the times," was Stephens' lofty rejoinder. "It is a common occurrence and is frequently done in the legislature and in Congress."

This did not convince Dr. Gunn, who departed and made report to the other Methodists. They voted to strike Stephens' name from the rolls of their church membership.

This excommunicatory action did not greatly injure Stephens, either in his feelings or in his attempts to make money. In 1868, he ran for the state senate, on the newly potent Republican ticket, but was defeated by Bedford Brown. Stephens then contested the election, pointing out that his opponent had served in the Confederate state legislature and was therefore ineligible, under the Fourteenth Amendment, to hold public office. Brown was excluded from the senate, a special election was called, and this time Stephens won.

As state senator, he was in a position to institute a number of grafting enterprises. He also became a justice of the peace, by appointment of the unspeakable Judge Albion W. Tourgée, who, in addition and for the sum of $20, issued Stephens a license to practise law.

His widowed mother, whom he had deserted in Rockingham County after embezzling her property, managed to follow him to Yanceyville. She was a pitiful creature, subject to epileptic seizures. On June 30, 1869, she was found with her throat cut to the very neck bone, and her son announced that she had fallen against the jagged edge of a broken chamber pot. A coroner's jury agreed with him, but several neighbors thought that a knife, and not a chamber pot, had killed the poor lady.

All this while he labored zealously to realize his proclaimed purpose of making money. As justice of the peace, he received a share of the fines and costs he assessed. His trials were conducted with a blend of fantasy and brutality that could hardly be matched outside the sittings of that Court of Oyer and Terminer which, at Salem in Massachusetts during the summer of 1692, sent nineteen men and women to the gallows for the crime of witchcraft. He was able to influence voters in favor of candidates less squeamish than Dr. Gunn about paying him for his efforts. Extortion was among his devices, and undercover work for Governor Holden at a salary of $7 a day plus expenses. He wielded a mighty influence with local members of the Union League, who repeatedly committed arson against Stephens' business and political rivals. He began modestly, with cow sheds and tobacco barns, but before he had finished he was credited with having ordered the burning of a Yanceyville hotel and a whole row of store buildings.

He frightened many people, but not all. The mordant Josiah Turner, then editing the anti-Holden Raleigh *Sentinel,* referred in his columns to the Caswell County politico as "Chicken" Stephens. Not only did the Conservatives delight thus to name him—the soubriquet was picked up by Stephens' own constituents. A. K. McClure, the Pennsylvania journalist, visited Yanceyville in 1868 and asked an audience of Negro voters about Stephens. Wilson Cary, sepia-brown and deservedly popular for ready wit, rose in the auditorium to reply.

"Mr. Stephens stole a chicken and was sent to the state senate," he informed McClure, amid howls of laughter throughout the hall, "and if he'd steal a gobbler he'd be sent to Congress."

Holden himself was heard to say, early in 1870, that Senator Stephens was a "clog to the party," and that a more respectable man should replace him in office. Various die-hard old Confederates in Caswell County, who dissented from almost every other taste and attitude expressed by Holden, agreed with him wholeheartedly concerning Stephens.

To such adverse opinions, no man trained to live by his wits could be unresponsive. Stephens was wealthy now, with a fine house and pocketfuls of fifty and hundred dollar bills which he liked to display, but these did not wholly comfort him when he reflected that enemies might be looking for him with something besides a telescope. In his bedroom he built an iron-barred cage, in which he slept with an arsenal of weapons around him. During his waking hours he carried knives and pistols, and he seemed highly nervous when anybody came suddenly close behind him.

On Washington's Birthday of 1870 he bought $10,000 worth of life insurance, and on April 7 he asked his friend Judge Tourgée to draw up a will for him, dividing his property equally among his wife and two daughters. Extraordinary precautions, these, for a healthy man only thirty-eight years old. The way he acted, one would imagine that he had no more than a few weeks left to live.

And he didn't.

The Ku Klux Klan of Reconstruction times was operating in North Carolina. This order, not to be confused with the twentieth-century disturbers of peace who filched the name and the sheeted regalia, was seen riding in the gloom of Yanceyville evenings—"those 'here today gone tomorrow' gentlemen with flowing white robes, those speechless spirits on milk-white steeds," they were described by A. J. Stedman, the Danbury editor. Most Caswell County citizens credited them with the midnight whipping of Chicken Stephens' brother-in-law and fellow agitator of Union Leaguers, James Jones, who promptly left the county. Stephens himself felt their presence strongly enough to write an appeal to Governor Holden. "We are unable to administer the laws," he complained, "unless you get our county under military rule."

Holden was planning something like that. He authorized the enlisting and equipping of state troops for active duty, under the command of a notable thief and destroyer named George W. Kirk. But this armed force was not ready for action when May 21, 1870, dawned unseasonably chilly, and a large but not quite usual Saturday crowd thronged the streets of Yanceyville.

In the Caswell County courthouse—it still stands, solid and architecturally interesting, a reminder of how well they built in 1785—plenty was going on. The courtroom on the second floor was occupied by some three hundred county Democrats in convention session. On the first floor, in the grand jury room, property owners declared their taxes to County Treasurer Arthur Hopkins and his deputies. Many county employees and visitors passed through the hallways and chambers. Outside in the square and along the streets beyond, crowds of people strolled, shopped, loafed, and conversed.

Former Sheriff Frank A. Wiley came to the front door of the courthouse. He attracted eyes wherever he went, for he was something like six feet eight inches tall, and powerfully built, with a massive head, shoulders wide enough to fill a door, and fists like huge cobblestones—altogether the most magnificent physical specimen in Caswell County. He talked to Hamp Johnson, a colored man, teasing him about a girl and asking his help in hitching a horse to a buggy. Then he strode up the stairs, two at a time, and entered the courtroom.

Senator Stephens also appeared, declared his taxes to Hopkins, and then followed Wiley to the convention. Several courthouse loafers now noticed a rather ominous gathering of stalwart figures around the outer steps—"stout-looking men," James Gunn described them later. None wore anything so conspicuous as Ku Klux regalia, but two revealed individuality in their garments; one had a white coat, trousers and hat, the other striped breeches and a yellow coat. Said a member of this group, "The people are weak to submit to Stephens" and looked significantly at his companions.

Stephens reached the convention in time to take copious notes on a speech by his erstwhile political rival, Bedford Brown. Since he was known as an informer for Governor Holden, he was assailed on all sides by scowling stares of cold dislike. However, he was thick-skinned enough to disdain such attention and made an end of his note-taking. Then he nudged Wiley, drew him aside, and in an undertone urged him to declare for sheriff on the Republican ticket.

To Wiley, a lifelong Democrat and an outspoken critic of Stephens and the whole Reconstruction regime, such a proposal must have been an insult. He glared at Stephens in utter amazement. Stephens insisted that he wanted to "harmonize political matters," and that for Wiley to change sides and seek office would greatly assist in such harmonization. Implicit in his words and manner was the offer of help, at a price, in winning the election.

Wiley told him that he could not and would not make such a campaign, and left the courtroom. Stephens followed him downstairs, still arguing. Several men were to remember seeing Wiley and Stephens at the foot of the staircase, at a few minutes past four in the afternoon. Later, Wiley was seen outside. Of Stephens, no subsequent glimpse was reported.

He had told his wife that he would return for supper at five o'clock. She waited for some time, with the food growing cold on the table. Then she remembered that Stephens had asked her, earlier in the day, if she knew where his life insurance policy was kept and had added the observation that it might be of value to her and the children. Though the remark had seemed banal enough when made, it now impressed the lady as significant and even frightening. She sent for her husband's brothers, W. H. and T. M. Stephens, who also lived in Yanceyville. At her request, these two went out to make inquiries.

They found nobody who could give them any news of their missing brother. The sun set, shortly before seven o'clock, and the searchers enlisted the aid of some county officials, who led them into the courthouse. Several rooms were visited and proved empty. At last the party stopped in front of a door next to the jury room where taxes had been declared.

This chamber, at the southeast corner of the building, had recently been used as headquarters for an agent of the anathematized Freedman's Bureau but had been vacated and used for the storage of wood for stoves in the various offices. It was now locked. M. W. Norfleet, clerk and master in equity for Caswell County, said that he had last seen the key in April, and that it must be in the possession of a Negro janitor.

Everyone went outside again. Night had fallen in the square. A dry goods box was brought from somewhere and set on the ground below the east window. One of the Stephens brothers mounted upon it with a burning candle. He peered through the glass pane and then stepped down, reporting that he could see nothing of interest.

Most of the searchers left, but several Negroes took up positions around the courthouse to watch. W. H. Stephens scaled a tree near the east window of the wood room and stayed there all night, like an owl. As Sunday morning dawned, the early light struck through the window almost under his nose, and he could see, inside the room, a silent prone body.

At once he called out, and others came to look. The window sash was raised, and they scrambled in.

Chicken Stephens lay huddled between two heaps of kindling. Around his neck had been drawn a noose of rope, so tightly that it had sunk deep into the flesh. His throat had been gashed on either side of the larynx, and a stab showed directly above his heart. On the floor lay a horn-handled pocket knife, its three-inch blade showing a trace of dried blood. Someone touched the body, and it was cold and stiff with rigor mortis.

Stephens had not been robbed. He wore his gold watch, and in his pockets was found a considerable sum of money. Missing, however, were the three pistols he was known to have carried. Flecks of dried blood sprinkled the sill of the east window. A smear showed on the ledge outside, and on the wooden box, still standing on the ground, could be seen the print of a thumb in blood.

The science of fingerprinting was not then so exact or so respected as to cause this box to be kept. However, a whirl of speculation beat up around it. Had Stephen's brother in the tree dozed? And had the dead man been lifted through the window from outside without being seen?

County officials decided that the murder must have taken place in the wood room itself, at some time between four and seven o'clock on the evening of May 21.

Coroner A. G. Yancey held an inquest, beginning that Sunday and continuing until Thursday, May 26. He examined some thirty-five witnesses and heard his jury declare that Chicken Stephens had come to his death "by the hands of some unknown person or persons." The newspapers whooped out the news. The Raleigh *Standard*, official organ of Holden's administration, was particularly voluble. It called the killing "a murder which should have been telegraphed from Paris to New York, or from Kamschatka to San Francisco," and on its own responsibility spent $50 in telegraphing from Raleigh to Washington, a long report of the affair to Congress. "The time will soon arrive," further editorialized the *Standard*, "when military aid will be the last resort in maintaining peace. We believe it is at hand now. Why should there be longer delay?"

More moderate were the two brothers of the dead man, who on June 2 published in the state newspapers their own statement:

"In view of the excited state of the public growing out of the late murder of our brother, J. W. STEPHENS, we deem it proper, with a view to its publication, to make the following statement in reference to the circumstances connected with this sad affair. A jury of inquest was empanelled on Saturday [*sic*] morning, shortly after the dead body was discovered, and were not discharged until the following Thursday afternoon. A large number of witnesses, both white and colored, were examined, which gave no clue to the perpetrator of this horrible deed. The officers of the law and the citizens of this community exhibited throughout a commendable zeal in endeavoring to ferret out the guilty party. Certain prominent individuals were at one time suspected of having some agency in the murder, the evidence however elicited during the examination satisfied us beyond a doubt of their innocence. We feel it to be our duty to state further, that from the evidence adduced during the investigation that we have not the slightest ground to suspect any citizen of this community of having any agency in the perpetration of this crime.

"Signed,

"W. H. STEPHENS

"T. M. STEPHENS"

But there were those who felt sure that the Caswell County Ku Klux Klan rode at the orders of Captain John G. Lea, twenty-seven-year-old Confederate veteran with a thick moustache and blazing gray eyes. He had been at the courthouse on the afternoon of the murder, and so had others of his alleged following.

Governor Holden, however he had yearned for the removal of Stephens, had not wanted to lose a henchman so dramatically. He commissioned Kirk a colonel of the North Carolina militia and directed him to raise a thousand state troops for active duty in Caldwell and Alamance counties. This command included some sincere Unionists from the mountains of Tennessee and North Carolina, a number of ruffians and mental defectives, and a good stiffening of professional gunmen and hoodlums from as far away as New York City. Dressed in blue uniforms such has had been worn by Sherman's invading Yankees, these raffish moss-troopers followed Kirk into Yanceyville on July 26. Their first act of any consequence was to arrest Lea, Wiley, J. T. Mitchell, and Felix Roan as prime suspects in the murder of Chicken Stephens.

Only Wiley, the towering giant who once had been sheriff in Caswell County, refused to submit with quiet dignity. He knocked down the first of Kirk's men to lay hands on him and fought so savagely against seven others that he was not shackled until someone had stunned him with a blow of a fence rail. The four were dragged to jail. Kirk refused to obey a writ of habeas corpus for their release and thereby laid the foundations for his own later prosecution for contempt. At Raleigh the four men were presented before the State Supreme Court.

It soon developed that their captors could offer no valid evidence against them, but only grumbled suspicions. They were promptly discharged by the court and emerged upon the streets of Raleigh into the midst of a noisy ovation that smacked of Mardi Gras. Bonfires were kindled, old cannon fired with cheerful roars, and a street parade went yelling through the town, with the four discharged prisoners carried shoulder high like heroes.

"They couldn't even prove there is a Ku Klux Klan in Caswell County," said a cheering admirer of Captain Lea, "let alone whether or not the Ku Klux did it." Whatever the legal proofs, however, several Reconstructionist officials in Caswell County had their own ideas about the existence of the order and its capabilities. Within twenty-four hours after Lea and his companions had returned from Raleigh, the Yanceyville heads of the Union League had packed and left for a quieter environment in Danville.

There was not much further effort on the part of Holden's satraps or Kirk's mercenaries. The election of the autumn of 1870 returned a majority of anti-Holden conservatives to the legislature. Holden was impeached and removed from office, and Kirk escaped imprisonment only by leaving the state.

Notably quiet among the celebrants of these happy matters was Captain James G. Lea, the reputed head of Caswell's Ku

Klux. In any case, orders had come from the Grand Wizard to disband the night-riding empire, and carpetbaggers and scalawags were fleeing in terror from North Carolina.

People asked Captain Lea about the Ku Klux Klan and about Chicken Stephens. He always shook his head. "You all can wait until I die," he said over and over again, and those who waited had a long time of it, for he lived to be ninety-two years old.

Former Sheriff Wiley died near Taylorsville in 1889, and the report spread that on his death bed he had confessed to a part in the murder of Stephens. His old friend, R. Z. Linney, who was beside that death bed, denied this.

"He made no reference to the Stephens tragedy," said Linney, but added that the spring before Wiley had spoken of that Saturday in Yanceyville, insisting that his last sight of Stephens was in the courthouse corridor and that he, Wiley, was four miles away from Yanceyville at the time when Stephens was said to have met his death.

In 1912, Captain Lea prepared a twelve-page typewritten memoir, signed and sealed it, and delivered it to the North Carolina Historical Commission, together with instructions that it be left unopened until his death. It was on September 27, 1935, that the gray-eyed old soldier died peacefully at his home in South Boston, Virginia, and the document was made public.

It is still a fascination to read.

Captain Lea confessed himself the founder, organizer, and chief of the Ku Klux Klan in Caswell County, as so frequently charged and never successfully confirmed or denied. Among his associates were all three of the men who were arrested with him on the charge of murdering Stephens.

They and others met one evening in the early spring of

1870, after considering the behavior of Stephens and agreeing that forbearance had ceased to be a virtue. They then organized as a court of law, complete with judge, prosecutor, and jury, and lacking only the physical presence of the defendant. They experienced no trouble or hesitation in finding Stephens guilty of treason, homicide, theft, and arson, and in pronouncing upon him the sentence of death.

Lea and his fellows, like W. S. Gilbert's logical Mikado, saw no moral difference between the dignified judge who condemns a criminal to die and the industrious mechanic who carries out the sentence. Having finished with enacting the roles of judge, prosecutor, and jury, they now took upon themselves the titles and duties of executioners.

On the morning of that fatal Saturday at the Yanceyville courthouse, Lea told his men to gather inconspicuously, no more than two or three together. They included J. T. Mitchell, James Denny, Joe Fowler, Tom Oliver, Pink Morgan, Dr. S. T. Richmond, Felix Roan, and others. The giant Wiley was already at the meeting of Democrats in the courtroom, and his was the assignment of bringing Stephens within the grasp of others. Meanwhile, someone produced the key to the wood room—Felix Roan had obtained it, some weeks before, from a Negro janitor named Calvin Miles. Singly and in pairs, the conspirators drifted unobserved into the room, until a full dozen waited there.

Down from the second floor came Wiley with Stephens, carelessly chatting. Wiley led his victim toward the wood room. As they reached the door, Lea appeared in the corridor with Mitchell, Denny, and Fowler. He waved his companions to follow Stephens inside, and waited while the door closed.

In the wood room, Stephens turned. He found himself looking into the muzzle of a Colt's Navy revolver aimed at him by Denny. Mitchell stepped close to him and searched him, taking away his three pistols. They told Stephens to sit down on the stacked wood and be quiet.

Denny went outside, where Lea and Wiley waited. Apparently Denny had been assigned to do the actual killing, but now he declared himself unable to carry out orders.

Wiley turned to Lea. The former sheriff's great stature made him a marked man in Yanceyville. "You must do something," he told Lea. "I am exposed unless you do."

Lea, made of sterner stuff than either Denny or Wiley, entered the room. Stephens got up from where he sat and came toward Lea, begging to be saved from what he most accurately suspected would be his prompt destruction. Lea recorded nothing that he said in reply. Quite probably he said nothing, but he must have made some sort of signal; for Mitchell came up behind Stephens, threw a noose of rope over his head, and drew it tight.

Effectively this cut off Stephens' jabbering pleas. Mitchell tripped him, let him fall heavily, and set a foot upon him while he pulled powerfully upon the rope to tighten the noose further.

Stephens struggled without avail. Mitchell's stout foot kept him clamped down. Around his prone body gathered Oliver, Morgan, Dr. Richmond, and Fowler. Oliver drew and opened his knife, stopped down, and stabbed Stephens in throat and chest. Then he dropped the knife, and all of them stood clear.

Chicken Stephens was dead.

Lea kept the whole proceedings wonderfully quiet. Even now he did not lose his nerve. He bade his companions leave, one at a time, to go out of the courthouse and head for a meeting place some distance away from town. The last man out of the wood room turned the key in the lock and brought it with him. Gathering again, they rode out of Yanceyville to County Line Creek. Into the water the key was thrown. Then, at Lea's direction, they took a solemn oath never to tell of what had happened.

After that, those of them who were arrested endured questioning, threats, and trial with supreme calm and plausability of manner. Even during the riot of celebration after their discharge from custody at Raleigh, they only shook their heads at questions.

So far as can be established, every man of those who assisted at the killing of Chicken Stephens subsequently led a life of the utmost respectability. Several held public office. To the detriment of the axiom that murder will out, the secret of the slaying was kept inviolate until John G. Lea died, last of his band.

Considered calmly, if such consideration is possible, the murder of Chicken Stephens appears to have been accomplished with a combination of skill, cool-headedness, and good fortune that brings it very close to the category of perfect crime. Governor Holden and his subordinates very soon ceased to hunt for the killers, but there were latter-day sleuths, laboring in the service of public record. Samuel A. Ashe, North Carolina's indefatigable annalist, tried for long to ferret out the truth. Claude G. Bowers, when he visited North Carolina in quest of information for his account of Reconstruction, *The Tragic Era*, made mighty efforts to do likewise. The gentle and erudite Dr. J. G. de Roulhac Hamilton, when he wrote of North Carolina's post-war epoch, attacked the mystery with all the verve of a scholar detective, and came close, but not quite close enough, to a solution.

Indeed, the feat of killing Chicken Stephens in a room of the Caswell County courthouse, when every adjoining hall and room brimmed with officials and citizens, when just outside the windows moved a great Saturday crowd, has some aspects that would have roused the admiration of that connoisseur of successful violence, Thomas De Quincey.

Yet, it may be suggested, Lea and the others acted with method in the seeming madness of their audacity. A crowd can be employed as shelter by any killer who knows his job and keeps his nerve. With so many people around and inside the building, comings and goings from the wood room may have drawn less notice. Beyond that, they had only to maintain their presence of mind and use silent weapons—a knife and a noose of rope—and make a swift, unostentatious getaway when the work was done.

9

Two Songs of the Scaffold

THE MOUNTAIN FOLK OF North Carolina are the most picturesquely individual, and the least knowledgeably appreciated, of the whole state.

From somewhere comes the impulse to laugh at them. It is an impulse best indulged from a safe distance. Only a few years ago, for example, if you called a mountain man "hillbilly," you got home from there the best and quickest way you could manage. Outsiders have thought of these people in terms of feuding, moonshining, laziness, and quaint superstitions, as set forth in the delightful cartoons of Paul Webb and Al Capp.

Simple the mountaineers are. Stupid they are not. Nor are they lazy. Let him who thinks otherwise go to wrest a living from a corn patch laboriously tufted upon a high rocky slope, to scale which is in itself a feat of acrobatics. One must be vigorous if only to walk the steep, shivery-high trails between cabin and cabin. The breed tends naturally toward tall spareness of body and reserved dignity of manner. Plain and poor the life can be, but hospitality is a characteristic. The axe and the rifle are employed with familiar skill that becomes almost instinct. And any human being born and reared among sky-climbing pinnacles and plunging, whispering valleys, thick-etted with trees and strung with flowers, must of sheer natural necessity respond to an environment of beauty and grandeur. Not all of them can speak of it with glib grace, but most of them feel it.

From such stock came Zebulon Vance, governor and sena-tor; Thomas Wolfe, who wrote epics; a baleful succession of outlaws in the grand tradition, from the Harpe brothers to Otto Wood; brave soldiers, such as those who obliterated the King's men on King's Mountain, and those who pointed the blood-boltered victorious advance of the South at Chicka-mauga.

Naturally and logically, men and women of such strength and assurance and pride have quarrelled and fought and killed. Between whiles, they have made songs. Sometimes the songs remember the violences.

The music itself is of the mountains. First into the high country came fiddles, because their shrill, vibrant melody frightened prowling wolves back from the campfires. The banjo followed, a ready borrowing from old minstrel shows. The guitar, once considered an artificial and ladylike instru-ment, has become popular only within the past score of years. But all three musics, alone or together, successfully interpret the stories of crimes long committed and expiated among the crags and hollows.

There are two in particular—the murder of Charles Silver on the Toe River in 1831, and the murder of Laura Foster in Happy Valley in 1866.

1. "For Now I Try That Awful Road"

THE KINK in Toe River comes on the line between Yancey and Mitchell counties, just about three miles west of Bakersville; but a century ago, there were no Yancey or Mitchell counties, nor yet a Bakersville. That part of the world still belonged to Burke County.

The names in that region hark back to tragedies and wars. Yancey's county seat, Burnsville, honors Captain Otway Burns who commanded a lively and destructive privateer during the War of 1812. The Toe River itself abbreviates its name from Estatoe, who was the daughter of an Indian chief far back in shadowy time. She tried to elope with her lover from another tribe, but his canoe swamped in the river and he drowned. Estatoe killed herself and became a romantic myth. Go southward from the place of her suicide and climb Mount Mitchell, and you cannot but remember Elisha Mitchell, who lost his life exploring that highest of North Carolina's peaks that properly bears his name.

But who Deyton was, for whom the kink in Toe River was named Deyton Bend, folks can't rightly tell you. Probably Deyton was an honorable man, the kind who is liked when he lives and forgotten when he dies. The memories around Deyton's Bend turn most readily to the spot where, in a long-vanished cabin among the grand heights and secret groves, happened a memorable murder. That is the sort of thing that stays in the mind, from generation to generation of the proud, thoughtful mountain dwellers.

Straight and circumstantial comes the story from those high places. It has the chill prod of winter gales, and the roar of a fire hotter and bigger and more officiously tended than is usual among decent law-abiding cabin-dwellers. And there is the blood-darkened secrecy of a jealous heart and the ungainsayable native wit of a gray old hunter who tracked down a killer as never he tracked deer or bear. Finally there is the bitter justice of the law's noosed rope, and to tell it all there is a quavering, echoing song of repentant sorrow.

But these are not imaginings. The court records are there, too, boldly informative.

It was in Deyton's Bend, at New Christmas time of 1831, that Charlie Silver suddenly hushed his singing and laughing and laid his lithe body down in death.

Cathcarts lived in the Bend region, and Sharpes and Cullises and Youngs, and the numerous enterprising brood of old John Silver. More lately, a family named Stewart had come up from the Anson County lowlands—"furriners," strangers were apt to be called in the mountains, whether they hailed from Anson County or Japan. The Stewarts built their cabin near the Silver farm.

John Silver had a son named Charlie, and Isaiah Stewart had a daughter named Frances. These two were bound to meet. It surprised nobody when they loved and married. Charlie Silver built a pole cabin down by the side of Toe River, just over the ridge from his father's home, and he and Frances Stewart Silver settled down.

Within the memory of living people, this bride and groom have been described by those who knew them well.

Charlie came from a family of personable men and women. Said his half-brother, late in the century: "He was strong, healthy, good-looking and agreeable. He had lots of friends. Everybody liked him." He was especially popular at the play-parties and working-bees of the district, because he could bear a helpful hand at raising barns or building fences, and when the work was finished and the fun began he "could make merry by talking, laughing and playing musical instruments." That is the sort of young mountain man who is the life of a party today.

Frances Silver—her kinfolks and her husband called her Frankie—"was a mighty likely little woman," said the same half-brother. "She had fair skin, bright eyes and was counted pretty. She had charms. I never saw a smarter little woman. She could card and spin her three yards of cotton a day on a big wheel."

These are the words of someone who lived to dislike her, and there is something grudging in the words "counted pretty." Others, interviewed in the 1930's by Muriel Earley Sheppard, spoke with eager eloquence of Frankie Silver's blonde beauty. The small, fair-haired, sweet-faced girl who could spin three yards of cotton a day, the strong, handsome country boy who was welcome at all the parties—they must have been a pair to admire. When they had been married a year, a daughter was born to them. They called her Nancy.

It was cold up in Deyton's Bend on December 22, 1831. Charlie wanted to sit by the fireplace and play with his baby daughter, but Frankie reminded him that he planned to go hunting on the morrow, and that there was not a great deal of firewood. He nodded brightly. Yes, he might be gone for several days. Taking the well-whetted axe from its corner, he walked out to where a hickory tree stood and skilfully felled it. With easy axeman's skill he hewed off the limbs, split the trunk, and finally reduced the whole pile to lengths that would fit in the fireplace. He racked up this wood, enough to last for a week. Then he came in to supper, and afterward dozed in the chimney corner with his little daughter cuddled in his arms.

On the next morning, December 23, Mrs. John Silver and

her two oldest daughters were in their yard, washing clothes. Over the ridge came Frankie.

"You're hard at it early," she praised her mother-in-law. "I've been at it myself since before day."

One of the Silver girls remarked appropriately. Perhaps she inquired after her brother, for Frankie said that Charlie had gone over the river to hunt, apparently heading for the home of his friend, George Young. She then departed, but she was back about sundown.

Charlie had not come back, she said, though she had expected him earlier. Mrs. Silver thought that Frankie seemed nervous over this absence. Frankie said that she would walk three-quarters of a mile to her father's home and spend the night there, if the Silvers could see to the feeding of Charlie's cow.

"Charles fed her this morning," she added.

At his mother's bidding, seventeen-year-old Alfred Silver went across the ridge and to Charlie's cow shed. He remembered later that he saw no tracks of his brother near the shed, only the marks of a woman's shoes.

Another day dawned and died. Charlie was not back at his home on Christmas Eve, nor on Christmas Day, when Frankie returned to the home of the Silvers, little Nancy in her arms. She was in no holiday mood.

"As he has remained away so long," she is reported as saying, with cold anger, "I do not care whether he comes back or not."

She went to stay at the home of Isaiah Stewart, returning to her own cabin only to gather up some clothing.

On December 26, the mountain men gathered to hunt for the missing Charlie.

Then as now, these were active, respectable men, wonderfully adroit in stalking and climbing. The mountain men of 1831 grew beards reminiscent of minor prophets or discoverers of new worlds. They wore home-tanned deerskin and home-woven wool. On their hairy lips hung words and phrases that reminded scholars of the speech of England in the days of great Elizabeth. By nature they were—they still are—invaluable friends and implacable enemies. In small groups they scoured the margins of Toe River and its tributary creeks, the slopes of Mitchell, Bee Ridge, the Black Brothers. And they found neither hide nor hair of Charlie Silver.

John Silver racked his brain for a hopeful inspiration. When the searching of his friends and relatives failed, he bethought him of something he'd heard about on the Tennessee side of the range. Some forty miles away, so rumor had come to him, lived a Negro "conjure-man," a slave belonging to somebody named Williams. Saddling his best horse, John Silver rode for two cold days over chancey trails and through narrow passes.

Williams made him welcome. The slave-magician was away from home just then, it developed, but the master had understudied methods of conjuration. He rummaged around to find the slave's prized instrument for divining secrets. It was a glass ball that hung from a cord. Williams suspended it above a sheet of paper on which Silver had made a rough map of the Deyton's Bend country.

The ball, said Williams, would swing to show in what direction Charlie Silvers had come to grief. The two watched, but could detect no slightest quiver of motion. The glass ball dangled at the end of its cord, directly above the mark that showed the position of Charlie's cabin.

"Wasn't it possible that the man was done away with at home?" asked Williams.

Silver thought not. Williams studied the map and the ball. "I think the body must have been found," he said.

Silver rode back home again, to learn that in his absence some highly interesting discoveries had been effected.

On the day that Silver had talked to Williams in Tennessee, searchers still prowled the hills and thickets of Deyton's Bend, while winter gales whipped around them with a note of shrill mockery. But one old neighbor picked up his staff and went to call on Frankie Silver, who had returned to her cabin.

This man was Jake Cullis, gray-bearded but wiry and bright-eyed. Even in that community of woodsmen, he was respected for his skill as hunter and trapper. Reaching the cabin, he did not enter at once, but made a slow, meditative circle of the yard. Then he came in and gazed into the fireplace. He thrust his staff into the great mass of dull ashes and stirred them around. Frankie watched with what may have been curiosity or resentment, or both, or another emotion.

"There are too many bits of bones in this fireplace," said Cullis quietly, "and the ashes are too greasy."

From the midst of the clutter on the hearth he raked out a pebble. He called for a bowl of water, and Frankie brought it. Carefully the old man slid the pebble in. It sank, and he watched. Bubbles rose, a whole dancing swarm of them.

"Grease bubbles," said Jake Cullis.

Neighbors gathered and watched. Frankie Silver said nothing, but she stood tense and pale. The old trapper walked out of the house, again quartered the yard with searching eyes and poking staff. Near the spring from which Frankie drew water was a hole, and into this he dug, pulling out clots of ashes. They rattled, those ashes. Stooping, Cullis fumbled out bits of bone, then something else. It was a small gridiron-shaped piece of metal like a buckle.

Several onlookers recognized that buckle. Charlie Silver had worn it, or its twin, on his hunting shoes.

Now Cullis stood aside. He said nothing, and he needed to say nothing. Others combed the ashes from the hole and the hearth. More bone fragments, and several teeth, came to light. Finally the floor by the fireplace was pulled away. The planks had been rigorously scrubbed, but on the earth below them showed a dark circular blotch of blood—"as big as a hog's liver," remarked one of the searchers.

Sheriff W. C. Butler was sent for. He listened to a great deal of fact, a great deal more of theory. Frankie Silver steadfastly denied having killed her husband, but the sheriff put her under arrest. The point was raised as to how she, small and slender, could have killed her stalwart husband and disposed of his body. She must have had help—her own family, perhaps. After asking more questions, Sheriff Butler arrested her mother and her brother Blackston, and brought them to the jail at Morganton on January 9, 1832.

No surviving record tells what attorneys represented these accused; but counsel they had, secured for them by Isaiah Stewart, who by January 13 was in Morganton to do what he could for his wife and children. Through his lawyers he protested that they were held in jail without legal trial or specific charge. Two justices of the peace, Thomas Hughes and J. C. Burgner, directed the sheriff to bring the three prisoners to a hearing on January 17. Barbara and Blackston Stewart—"Stuart," the name was spelled on the judgment notice—impressed the justices so favorably that they were set free on bonds of one hundred pounds, English money, each, to appear at the March term of court in Morganton.

On March 17, a grand jury considered an indictment and dropped all charges against Barbara and Blackston Stewart, but returned a true bill against Frankie, who pleaded not guilty. Her trial was set for March 29. Fully 150 jurors were summoned, a number that indicates the breadth as well as the height of interest in the case and its principals.

William Alexander appeared as solicitor. Research by the painstaking Clifton T. Avery of Morganton, whose study of the case spread over a number of years, leads him to suggest that the defendant may have been represented by D. J. Caldwell, Joseph McDowell, or Isaac T. Avery, all of whom were practising law in Burke County in 1832.

The presentation of testimony began on the morning of March 29, before Judge John R. Donnell. A principal witness was Jake Cullis, solemn, weighty, a bearded figure of nemesis. Exhibits were offered—the bits of charred bone, the teeth, the iron buckle, the axe that showed dulled and notched by chopping something harder than hickory wood. The defense presented evidence in its turn, though what was the nature of that evidence cannot be surely established today. It was candle light when the case went to the jurymen, who deliberated all night and then returned to the courtroom to say that they had not yet agreed upon a verdict. They wanted to question some of the witnesses on specific points.

Judge Donnell summoned the witnesses called for, and to these various members of the jury directed their questions. Counsel for the prisoner objected to this procedure, reminding that the witnesses had been kept apart during the trial but since the end of argument had been permitted to mingle perhaps to discuss the matter.

"Such is the case," said Judge Donnell, in substance, in his new charge to the jury, "but it could not have been anticipated that you would wish to hear any of the witnesses examined again after the case had been put to you and you had retired from the bar; but the jury ought to hear the witnesses without prejudice arising from the circumstances of their having had an opportunity of being together since their former examination."

The jury retired once more, and later in the day appeared to pronounce Frankie Silver guilty of murder as charged. Defense council moved for a new trial. Judge Donnell overruled the motion, and Solicitor Alexander asked for immediate pronouncement of judgment. In set and dignified terms, the judge spoke as he must speak:

"It is the sentence of this court that the prisoner, Frances Silver, be taken back to the prison from whence she came and there to remain until the last Friday of July court next of Burke County, and then to be taken from thence to the place of public execution, and then and there to be hung by the neck until she be dead."

This was the first sentence of death ever to be invoked against a woman in the entire history of North Carolina as a state. Frankie's lawyers appealed to the State Supreme Court and secured for their client a stay of sentence while decision was being handed down.

Their appeal was based upon the matter previously protested, the questioning of witnesses after such witnesses had been permitted to mingle. The Supreme Court found no error in the trial. Burke County officials were directed to proceed to judgment and sentence of death against Frankie Silver, and costs of the appeal were assessed against her father and her brother Jackson as her sureties.

The hanging had been set for the fall term of court, and when September came to Burke County, Judge D. L. Swain had been assigned to preside. But September of 1832 was a phenomenally busy month for this brilliant young jurist who, by December, would take office as the youngest governor in North Carolina history. When he failed to appear to open court, Sheriff Butler declared court adjourned until the spring of 1833. That meant six months more of life for Frankie Silver.

She did not want to spend those six months in Burke County's dim and cramping jail, with death waiting at the end. Her loyal relatives were ready to help her get out. One of her brothers, a skilful wood carver, visited her and made an intent study of the keyhole of the lock on her cell door. That survey was enough to enable him to whittle from hard wood a key that would let her out. This key was smuggled into Frankie's hands, and one night she escaped.

Another kinsman, an uncle, was waiting outside. He handed her a suit of men's clothes and a broad hat, and with this under her arm she burrowed into the hay that filled his wagon. There she slipped out of her dress and pulled on shirt, trousers, and coat. Then her uncle cut away her flowing blonde hair. When the wagon rolled out of Morganton at dawn, she strolled behind it, like a farm boy heading for home.

Burke County had a new sheriff, John Boone, said to be a nephew or grand-nephew of immortal Daniel. Hot on the trail of the fugitive Sheriff Boone led a posse of mounted deputies. They caught up with the wagon too suddenly for Frankie to hide herself in the hay. Boone rode close up beside her.

"Frances," he said.

"Thank you, sir, my name is Tommy," she replied, as deeply and steadily as she could.

"Yes, her name is Tommy," volunteered the uncle, who

must have come from the dim-witted side of the Stewart family.

"*Her* name?" repeated Boone, and snatched the hat from Frankie's head.

Back to jail he led her, and also locked up the uncle and her father on charges of aiding a prisoner to escape. They obtained their freedom shortly after the first of June.

At spring court, the date for her hanging was set for June 28, but she won another delay, until July 12. In the meantime, she was allowed to receive visitors in her cell. Among them was a woman from Deyton's Bend, a neighbor she knew and liked. To this friend, Frankie Silver unburdened her wretched soul, first exacting an oath of silence until after the hanging.

Frankie had been jealous of her husband—she had thought he paid too much attention to other women at those parties where he was always so welcome. On December 22, 1831, she had asked him to cut a week's supply of wood.

That night he dozed in front of the fire with his little daughter in his arms. Frankie stooped and gently eased the child out of his slack grasp, carried her across the room and laid her on a bed. Frankie then picked up the axe, lifted it with both hands above her head, and brought it down with all her strength.

It was a terrible blow, striking deep into Charlie's neck, but he sprang to his feet. "God bless the child!" he cried out loudly.

Frankie ran to the bed and hid her face in the quilt. She heard her husband fall and thrash around miserably. Then she rose, caught up the axe again, and struck a second and finishing blow. After that, she hacked Charlie's body into pieces, built up the fire and began to burn him, a joint at a time, on the hearth.

It was an all-night task, and she used every stick of the wood he had cut that day. When it was gone, she went into the yard to smash up the front steps and an old dog house. Between whiles she scrubbed the bloody floor with water and a broom of twigs. By morning she felt sure that Charlie Silver had vanished forever from the sight and mind of men.

On July 12, a pleasant day with bright sunshine, she was led forth to die. According to the grim custom of the time, the scaffold had been set up in public. "There was a sight of folks to see her hanged," remembered a man who helped swell the throng. Frankie Silver, they said, was a handsome woman as she mounted the steps with a preacher at her side.

The hangman stationed himself at her elbow. She looked at him and made a gesture, then stepped slightly forward and faced the throng. Some thought she was going to speak, to confess.

In the forefront of the spectators, a big man raised his face. It was Isaiah Stewart, her father and head of the clan, who had gained release from jail.

"Die with your secret, Frankie!" he yelled.

She bowed her head slightly and stepped back again. The black sack tightened around her throat. She died with no last words. Many who watched agreed that her neck was too pretty to be broken like that.

In and out through the crowd moved peddlers, selling sheets of printed paper. They contained a string of verses, speaking in the name of Frankie Silver and believed by many to have been written by her own hand as she sat waiting for her day of execution. A strong tradition has persisted that she actually recited these verses from the scaffold, but it is apocryphal. The language of the ballad is somewhat labored, but there is circumstantiality in it.

On one dark and dreary night
I put his body out of sight.
To see his soul and body part,
It strikes with terror to my heart.

I took his blooming days away,
Left him no time to God to pray,
And if sins fall on his head,
Must I not bear them in his stead?

The jealous thought that first gave strife
To make me take my husband's life,
For days and months I spent my time
Thinking how to commit this crime.

. . . .

His feeble hands fell gently down,
His chattering tongue soon lost its sound.
My mind on solemn subjects rolls,
My little child—God bless its soul;
All you that are of Adam's race,
Let not my faults this child disgrace.

Farewell, good people, you all now see
What my bad conduct brought on me;
To die of shame and disgrace
Before this world of human race.

Awful, indeed, to think of death,
In perfect health to lose my breath;
Farewell, my friends, I bid adieu,
Vengeance on me must now pursue.

Great God! How shall I be forgiven?
Not fit for earth, not fit for Heaven,
But little time to pray to God,
For now I try that awful road.

Frankie's body was turned over to her father and brothers.
One story says that they dug several graves on the way from
Morganton to Deyton's Bend, and that these were filled and
mounded on the day following the execution. Meanwhile, as
most chroniclers agree, she was buried near the old Buck-
horn Tavern, nine miles west of Morganton. A marker was
placed at the supposed spot in 1952 and may be passed by
travellers along Highway 105.

In 1836, the Court of Common Pleas placed little orphaned
Nancy Silver under guardianship of her grandmother, Barbara Stewart.

The Stewarts themselves had not long to survive as a family.
Isaiah Stewart was cutting down a tree for fence rails one day.
It fell upon him, smashing his skull. Barbara Stewart died
not long afterward, in agony from the bite of a huge mountain rattlesnake. Jackson Stewart, Frankie's brother, was
killed during the Civil War. Joe Stewart also died suddenly
and somewhat mysteriously. Blackston, once accused of having helped murder Charlie Silver, was hanged in Kentucky for
horse stealing.

"It looks like God made way with them on purpose,"
commented Alfred Silver in his old age. "I believe that all
conspired to kill Charles. It was a horrible deed! He was
such a fine fellow; we loved him."

One witness to the murder survived, Nancy Silver, who
as a baby may have wondered why her mother swung that
shiny thing in the firelit air, and why her father made such

funny noises as he grovelled on the floor. She grew to womanhood and married David W. Parker, who marched off to
Virginia with the 6th North Carolina Regiment in 1861 and
fell in the forefront of battle at First Manassas. She married
again and is said to have lived past her ninetieth birthday in
Madison County.

There remains to assess Frankie Silver's reason for murdering her husband. "That crocodile of vices," says James A.
Turpin in discussing Frankie's mad jealousy. There was gossip,
but only gossip, concerning Charlie Silver's supposed amorous
adventures with other men's wives, including one with the
impossible name of Mrs. Zeb Cranberry. No such charges
were made in any of the court actions. Once more, Alfred
Silver is quotable: "Nobody ever imagined that she had cause
to be jealous, for Charles was true to her. He laughed and
talked with the women of his acquaintance, but that was all."

If the people concerned died, by axe or scaffold or fall of
tree or bite of snake, the ballad of Frankie Silver survived.
Some mountain fiddler or banjoist set the verses to music with
a woeful minor strain. When Mrs. Sheppard visited the Toe
River in the 1930's, hunting material for her book *Cabins in
the Laurel,* she heard the song from time to time. She was
impressed with its melodic pattern—". . . an eerie, mournful
tune whose urgent minor beat is the restless scurrying of
unlaid ghosts in lonely places." But the tactful singers took
care never to voice it when members of the Stewart or Silver
families were near at hand. Perhaps that is why it is almost
never heard today.

2. *"Bow Your Head, Tom Dula"*

THE CIVIL WAR was over, in Wilkes County as in a lot of other places, and some of those who had marched away marched back again. Among these lucky ones was handsome young Tom Dula, who lived in Happy Valley and, you may be sure, had every reason to be happy.

He had served with the 26th North Carolina Regiment, and few indeed had returned from the decimated ranks of that repeatedly battered unit. The 26th had been raked with fire at New Bern, hideously punished at Malvern Hill. It had been almost wiped out at Gettysburg, where of all the regiments in Pickett's bloody charge it suffered worst. After that, it never mustered at anything like regimental strength again. Once, in the Wilderness, it went into battle only thirty-five strong, and of those, thirty-one were killed and wounded before sundown. The ninety-odd who surrendered at Appomattox were mostly late recruits.

Courage is a relative characteristic, and to say that Tom Dula won a reputation for soldierly daring among those of the 26th who lived to tell of it is to say at once that he was a hero. He fought hard and frequently and well, and he was never even wounded. If General Bryan Grimes had scowled death away, Tom Dula had smiled death away; it was like the old tale hunters told, about how Davy Crockett grinned the raccoon out of the tree.

Home he came, with his parole in his pocket, to the slopes above the Yadkin. Happy Valley had its contrasts, cultural and ethical as well as scenic. Vividly, even luridly, these contrasts were set forth by a contemporary journalist:

"The community . . . is divided into two entirely separate and distinct classes. The one occupying the fertile lands adjacent to the Yadkin River and its tributaries is educated and intelligent, and the other, living on the spurs and ridges of the mountains, is ignorant, poor and depraved. A state of immorality unexampled in the history of any country exists among these people, and such a general system of free-lovism prevails, that it is 'a wise child that knows its father.' "

One must take note that these words were written by a northern correspondent for the New York *Herald* and remember the tendency of outsiders, already here recognized, to misjudge North Carolina's mountain folk. Not all the cove-dwellers above Happy Valley were unlettered, for one Bob Cummings was a school teacher among them. Poverty they may have known, for the land was poor and sometimes almost perpendicular, but they worked that land and from it gained their living. That many of the community were personable and bold will shortly be demonstrated. As to what the *Herald's* representative referred to as "free-lovism"—well, Tom Dula was back home, and he liked the girls and the girls liked him.

He was a good-looking young man in his early twenties. Nearly six feet tall, with dark eyes and dark curly hair, he moved gracefully, paid smiling compliments, and he was a fiddle-scraping, banjo-picking caution. These were gifts of appearance and talent well calculated to stimulate feminine interest. Tom Dula began his conquests on a sensibly modest scale, with Laura Foster, the pretty but more than formally hospitable daughter of Wilson Foster.

Laura Foster was blue-eyed and chestnut-haired and hot-blooded. She had met other men of Happy Valley half-way, or perhaps closer than that. Indeed, it was considered something of a phenomenon that Schoolmaster Bob Cummings had admired her to no avail whatever. He was small and lean, and had been a conspicuous rule-proving exception to the way Laura lavished her favors on suitors.

Tom Dula was back from the war late in April or early in May of 1865, and probably he won Laura Foster's heart that same sweet summer—"courtin' summer," mountain folk sometimes say as young couples stroll along a trail, hand in hand. Like many another flighty damsel, Laura settled down solidly to a singleness of affection. Other young men who came calling found themself no more warmly welcome than Bob Cummings. Laura wanted Tom Dula, and nobody else.

That Lothario of the laurel thickets proved to be by no means so single of heart. Laura Foster he continued to meet, flatter, and fondle, but his great natural talents for romantic adventure found outlet in several other directions. One of those who melted before his smile was Pauline Foster, Laura's cousin. Possibly it was through Laura that Tom met Pauline; quite probably it was through Pauline that Tom met Ann Melton.

Here, certainly, was a woman who at first sight would make a man's mouth go dry to its roof and his eyes protrude like door knobs.

The *Herald* correspondent, quoted above to the reputational detriment of Happy Valley's upper slopes, was plainly a great judge of women's good looks. "Beautiful," he said unequivocally of Ann Melton, and went on to ascribe to her "... the manners and bearing of an accomplished lady, all the natural powers that should grace a high born beauty." This paragon, who on the word of others beside him of the *Herald* would have been the reigning belle of a far larger and more sophisticated population, was the more remarkable for her elegance in that she was totally illiterate. It becomes increasingly evident that she had a fine natural mind, and the characteristic presence and pride of a surpassing mountain beauty. She was married, but her husband, James Melton, is only a name in the record. Perhaps he was such a complaisant husband as were convenient for court ladies of earlier centuries. If he was not, it made no difference. Not to Ann Melton or Tom Dula.

In addition to beauty and poise, Mrs. Melton possessed land and money. She employed Pauline Foster as a servant in 1865 and early in 1866, and Tom Dula, visiting the maid, must have dallied with the mistress. He had no great wealth; for, like some other soldiers, he returned from fighting with no great appetite for working. But by early spring of 1866 he was solidly established in the affections of lovely Ann Melton. She loved him, or so folks said along the coves. That he loved her, too, was to be proved to everyone's satisfaction. Thus, in some ten months of brilliant campaigning, he had succeeded with Laura Foster, her cousin Pauline, and the incomparable Ann Melton. If love of women is wealth, as insists an old, old song, then Tom Dula had a virtual embarrassment of riches.

May came to the mountains, bright with flowers and balmy with warmth. On the 25th of that month, Wilson Foster wakened to call his daughter, and she was not in her bed. Absent, too, was a brown mare named Betty, which had been tethered in the yard.

A search of Laura's room showed that she had packed her clothes. An elopement? Wilson Foster and his sons suspected that. Or Laura may have gone visiting relatives in Watauga County, though why so secretively nobody could suggest. But days went by, and no news came of what had befallen her.

If Laura had eloped, it was to be wondered who her bridegroom might be. Her favored swains, with Tom Dula high at the head of the list, still labored or lounged above Happy Valley. Wilson Foster and his sons inquired and searched, with no success whatever.

It was three weeks later, on June 10, that someone led a gaunt brown mare to the Cowles store at Elkville.

"Found her tied to a tree, up at the Bates place," said the man. "She'd gnawed off the bark. Was tied up a right smart of time."

The Bates place was no residence, but a thickly wooded section, popular as a lovers' rendezvous. And somebody identified the mare as Foster's Betty.

Word flew over the ridges and down the coves. Men dropped tools or fishing rods or moonshine jugs and formed up into search parties. Everywhere they scoured, up slope and down hollow, staring into brown pools, peering behind logs, prying up rocks.

Near the spot where Betty had been tied, the brush showed a trampled disorder, as by a violent struggle. In widening circles around that point rode a party of searchers. A mile and a half away, a horse shied and snorted. Dismounting, the men prodded here and there until they found a grave hidden in a thick tangle of laurels.

They fetched spades and picks, and dug. Among them was Bob Cummings, the teacher who had courted Laura with so little encouragement. Soon enough earth had been scooped away to reveal a rotting body. It was no treat to see. Even veterans of corpse-cluttered battlegrounds stepped back nervously.

"That's Laura," volunteered Cummings, and several turned to look at him sharply.

"Look at the color of her hair," said Cummings.

It was chestnut, all right.

"That's her dress."

Several recognized the dress.

"Laura had a gold tooth on the left upper side of her mouth."

The account does not say who checked for the gold tooth, but it was there.

The diggers opened the grave the rest of the way. Laura Foster lay doubled and twisted. Both her legs had been broken, as though to make them fit into the short hole hastily dug to hide her. A deep stab had pierced Laura's once delectable bosom, penetrating to the heart. Under her lay a parcel of clothes, the baggage she had flung over Betty's saddle.

The body was carried to Elkville, and there Coroner G. A. Carter held inquest and performed an autopsy. Cummings was a witness at that hearing and was listened to with attention that varied from the admiring to the suspicious.

"This murder was done by someone we have known and trusted," he said bluntly. "He may be standing among you at this moment. Let's investigate as fully as possible until the law arrives."

Then he turned and walked away. There was a real consequence in his manner and movement. One or two, remembering how Laura Foster had scorned him, wondered if he might not know considerably more than he had told about how she came to be killed. They followed him to the Elk Creek farmhouse where he boarded and were told that he had packed some clothes as for a journey. Taking up his trail, they followed him straight back to the opened grave among the laurels.

He faced them and held out something. "It is the knife that stabbed her to death," he said.

Tom Dula had been at Cowles' store when Laura's body was carried in, and his handsome face had scowled fearsomely.

"I will have vengeance on whoever killed her," he announced sternly. Next day he was gone from Happy Valley.

But another former suitor of Laura, Jack Keaton, had likewise fled. When it came to that, Bob Cummings, so glibly the amateur detective at grave and inquest, had vanished. So had Jack Adkins, and so, too, had Ben Ferguson. You could take your choice about who was guilty, and why. Sheriff W. G. Hix was baffled about where to start looking for anybody.

Weeks passed, and then he need look no farther than Happy Valley.

In mid-July, the loafers who whittled and spat in front of the Cowles store saw a cavalcade of five horsemen amble into Elkville. At the head of the party rode little Bob Cummings, grim, tense, and triumphant. Jack Adkins and Ben Ferguson carried rifles and guarded the other two riders, each tied to his saddle. The prisoners were Tom Dula, smiling as usual, and Jack Keaton.

"I will charge these men with murdering Laura Foster," announced Cummings, almost stuffily triumphant, "and I also ask the arrest of Mrs. James Melton."

It turned out that Cummings and his two friends had traced Dula and Keaton to a hiding place in Tennessee. Cummings had written an adequate simulation of a writ of extradition, and they had handed it to Tennessee officers, who arrested the pair and turned them over to the North Carolinians. Keaton stared pallidly at his neighbors, but Dula, that gay smiler at disaster, seemed more good-humored than ever. He asked that his hands be freed. Then he unslung a fiddle from the saddle he rode and upon it scraped a lively tune for the gaping crowd. A deputy sheriff came to escort him and Keaton to Wilkesboro. A day later, Ann Melton was also locked up.

Keaton, more doleful about his arrest than Dula, proved more fortunate as well. He was able to prove an alibi and was set free, while Ann Melton and Tom Dula were bound over to the fall term of court on a murder charge. Into Wilkesboro then rode a striking figure, burning-eyed and fierce-moustached, who was immediately recognized and loudly cheered from both sides of the street.

Zebulon Baird Vance, thirty-six years old in 1866, was one of North Carolina's heroes. He had organized the 26th North Carolina Regiment in 1861 and had served as its first colonel while Tom Dula was a rookie private. Vance resigned his colonelcy in 1862 to become governor, but he had never lost his love and concern for the brave, bullet-torn 26th. Arrested by the victorious Federals at the close of the war, he had been released on parole and had been practicing law in Charlotte. When word came of Dula's arrest, Vance had packed his saddle bags. Hang one of the 26th? Not if Zeb Vance could prevent it. He announced himself as counsel for Dula and asked that his client be tried separately from Ann Melton, whose presence in a courtroom Vance judged to be a potential danger to any defendant except herself. He succeeded in gaining a change of venue to Statesville in Iredell County. Solicitor Walt Caldwell, who was preparing the case for the state, seemed in danger of being devoured alive by the fiery and picturesque Vance.

But the solicitor was talking quietly to Cummings, who explained, step by step, his case against Dula.

Cummings had coaxed a confidence from Mrs. Betsy Scott, a laundress, who had seen Laura an hour or so after she had ridden from home early on the morning of May 25. Laura had sat brown Betty without a saddle, holding a sack of clothing in front of her. She had told Mrs. Scott that she was heading for the Bates place, and that she intended to meet Tom Dula there and go with him to be married. Hearing this story, Cummings had paid Mrs. Scott to keep it a secret until he called for it to be told. Meanwhile, would Mrs. Scott spy on Ann Melton, while doing laundry at her home? Mrs. Scott would, and did, and it was through her that Cummings heard of Dula's hiding place in Tennessee. As to Cummings' reason for all this relentless trailing—"I loved her," he said of Laura Foster.

Dula went to trial before Judge Ralph Buxton, at the fall term of court. Vance had procured as associate counsel Judge R. F. Armstrong and R. P. Allison, and these did their best to shake the circumstantial evidence brought against Dula. Cummings was excoriated for his highly irregular methods in making the arrest. The testimony of Betsy Scott was challenged and attacked.

One telling piece of information established a motive for Dula. He had suffered from venereal disease, and blamed this upon Laura Foster. He had declared, in the hearing of several, that he would "put through whoever gave it to me."

Nobody seems to have noticed the similarity in Dula's alleged decoying of Laura by promise of elopement and marriage to the case of Jonathan Lewis's murder of Naomi Wise fifty-two years previously. Yet there may have been more than coincidence to explain that similarity. The song of Naomi Wise was a popular one in the mountains and elsewhere. Dula, skilled at banjo and fiddle, undoubtedly knew it by heart. It may have impelled him to imitation.

Vance objected to much of the testimony as merely hearsay. Finally, standing before the jury, he pleaded in heart-stirring periods for his client's life.

"I have known Tom Dula during years of strain and stress, when a man's soul was tried," he vowed at the top of his resonant and expressive voice, "and I tell you in all sincerity that never did a better soldier live, and never did one action of his ever lead me to believe him capable of murder."

There were ex-Confederates on the jury, and chiefly to them did Vance address himself when he recalled the desperate days of war.

"Is there a man among you," he wound up, "with a spark of love for the Lost Cause but can see that even if Tom Dula killed this lewd woman, Laura Foster—this minion of the devil—that the life of this man, who fought for what he thought best for your family and mine, is worth a hundred lives of such women as that dead viper."

Apparently twelve men disagreed with Vance as to the logic of this suggestion. Tom Dula was found guilty of murder in the first degree and was sentenced to hang.

Vance appealed to the State Supreme Court, urging in particular that a great deal of Mrs. Scott's evidence was only hearsay and therefore incompetent.

"The case discloses a most horrible murder," Chief Justice Richmond M. Pearson wrote the resulting opinion, "and the public interest demands that the perpetrator of the crime should suffer death; but the public interest also demands that the prisoner, even if he be guilty, shall not be convicted, unless his guilt can be proved according to the law of the land." A new trial was ordered, and in January, 1868, Dula faced another jury.

Again the charges, again Vance's earnest defense, and this time more evidence, damning both to Dula and to Ann

Melton. There were those who told that Dula and Ann had conferred earnestly on the day before Laura Foster's disappearance, and that Ann had given her lover a canteen full of whiskey—to heighten his courage, it was implied. And on the day when Laura was seen riding toward the Bates place, Ann was reported to have been absent from home for hours, returning with wet dress and shoes, to lie on her bed as though exhausted.

As before, the verdict was guilty. Vance's new appeal to the Supreme Court was unsuccessful. The hanging was set for May 1, 1868.

Meanwhile, Ann Melton's trial still remained to be held, after several delays. Zebulon Vance declared his earnest belief that she, and she alone, was guilty of the murder, and that his client and friend was sacrificing his life for her. On April 30, when Tom Dula had but a few hours of life left to him, his mother sent a letter begging him to make full confession. Dula seemed unmoved. He declined the spiritual comfort offered by a Methodist preacher but asked for pencil and paper. Awkwardly he scrawled a few lines:

"Statement of Thomas C. Dula: I declare that I am the only person that had a hand in the murder of Laura Foster."

He did not write his name at the bottom, only the date, April 30, 1868. This note he handed to R. P. Allison, one of his lawyers. Then he ate a hearty supper, joking the while with his jailer.

His last night was spent in more writing and in pacing the floor of the cell. By morning he had completed a longer document, fully fifteen pages of autobiographical musings. Probably it would be worth reading, and, in one or two opinions, even more worth destroying. Destroyed it was, or lost, like that other life history written by the Reverend Mr. George

Washington Carawan, and North Carolina's archives are poorer by two fascinating documents.

May Day had dawned, bright and beautiful. Dula declared himself ready to receive baptism, and the minister whose company he had previously rejected came to perform the rite. Sheriff Wasson led Dula from his cell just before noon. Crowds had gathered, including large numbers of young women. The solemnity of the occasion was recognized by a special police order closing all saloons and bars.

The *Herald* reporter, on whom this account has previously depended for several descriptions, had a good look at the prisoner as he appeared in the open and telegraphed his impressions to New York. "He fought gallantly in the Confederate service," said the dispatch, "where he established a reputation for bravery, but since the war closed, has become reckless, demoralized and a desperado, of whom the people in his community had a terror. There is everything in his expression to denote the hardened assassin—a fierce glare of the eyes, a great deal of malignity, and a callousness that is revolting."

Desperado was probably too harsh a word to apply to Dula. Assassin he was, on his own confession, but people had liked him and liked him still. The glare in his eyes, not too surprising for a man long jailed and now without hope, quickly faded. For Tom Dula was smiling. Out here in the streets of Statesville waited an old acquaintance of his, one whom he had greeted with other smiles on the slopes of hills called Malvern and Cemetery, and death was that acquaintance's name.

A wagon waited, with a coffin upon it. Into the wagon climbed Dula, and upon the coffin he sat. With him rode the sheriff, the minister, and his sister and brother-in-law. One account says that he tuned and played his fiddle, but the invaluable *Herald* representative records nothing so frivolous. Instead, he reports Dula as assuring his friends and relatives that he had truly repented of his crime. He rode, rather like a hero, between thronged curbs until he reached the depot. In front of that structure Sheriff Wasson had caused to be erected a scaffold of mountain pine, two stout uprights with a crossbar.

Thousands pressed close, men and boys climbing trees for a better view. A hollow square of armed deputies surrounded the scaffold as the wagon halted beneath it. Now Sheriff Wasson told Dula that he might speak to the crowd if he so desired.

To that invitation Tom Dula responded with hearty relish. He addressed the waiting citizenry in a voice that rang among the trees and echoed from the buildings. One may mourn that his remarks have survived only by indirect quotation in the columns of the *Herald*:

"He spoke of his early childhood, his parents, and his subsequent career in the army, referred to the dissolution of the Union, made blasphemous allusions to the Diety, invoking that name to prove assertions that he knew were, some of them at least, false. The politics of the country he discussed freely, and upon being informed, in reply to a question of his, that Holden was elected Governor of North Carolina, he branded that person as a secessionist and a man that could not be trusted. His only reference to the murder was a half explanation of the country and the different roads and paths leading to the scene of the murder, in which his only anxiety was to show that some two or three of the witnesses swore falsely against him. He mentioned particularly one, James Isbell, who he alleged had perjured himself in the case, and concluded by saying that had there been no lies sworn against him he would not have been there."

This address, which lasted nearly an hour, must have rambled extensively but was heard with the utmost attention. When Dula had finished, the time was past two o'clock. He took an affectionate farewell of his sister. Sheriff Wasson lowered the noose over his curly head, and he made a last joke.

"You have such a nice clean rope," he observed, "I ought to have washed my neck."

The noose drawn tight, the horses were whipped up and the wagon was yanked from under Tom Dula's feet. He dropped only a short distance, and his neck was not broken. He did not struggle as he dangled and strangled to death. Dr. Campbell pronounced him dead about 2:30, and his body was cut down and given to his relatives.

Meanwhile, mountain fashion, folks started to sing about him, in terms affecting enough:

> Oh, bow your head, Tom Dula,
> Oh, bow your head and cry;
> You've killed poor Laura Foster
> And you know you're bound to die.

> I take my banjo this evening,
> I pick it on my knee;
> This time tomorrow evening
> 'Twill be no use to me.

> I had my trial at Wilkesboro,
> Oh, what do you reckon they done?
> They bound me over to Statesville
> And there's where I'll be hung.

. . . .

Oh, pappy, oh, pappy,
What shall I do?
I have lost all my money
And killed poor Laura, too.

Oh, mammy, oh, mammy,
Bow your head and cry.
I've killed poor Laura Foster
And I know I'm bound to die.

Oh, what my mammy told me
Is about to come to pass;
That drinking and the women
Would be my ruin at last.

As in the case of Frankie Silver, the rumor grew into a legend that the condemned murderer had composed a confession in form of a personal death-ballad. Less melodramatic is the truth—the author was Thomas C. Land, a school teacher like Bob Cummings. The ballad was widely sung, and several versions are quoted in collections of folk songs. One of these erroneously calls it a ballad brought from England.

Ann Melton was still alive, and at last she came to trial. She made a beautiful and demure defendant, probably in the tradition of that other Ann, lovely Mrs. Simpson of Fayetteville. Dula's statement of exoneration worked greatly in her favor. A jury found her not guilty.

Tom Dula might have said words to convict her, neighbors have said since, but he was quiet because he loved her.

Years later, she was fatally injured when a wagon overturned upon her. It was sworn that, on the night she died, the room filled with a crackling sound as of burning meat, and a black cat was seen to climb the wall. Happy Valley dwellers have been persuaded to think that Satan came in person to escort Ann Melton to hell.

Laura Foster's poor broken body lies in an unmarked grave. It is hard to locate that grave on the brightest of summer days in Happy Valley.

But a few of the oldest residents say that the best time to go looking for it is at night. Midnight. Then Laura Foster's ghost will come gliding toward you, and she'll point out the very place if you care to wait and look.

Acknowledgments and Sources

MANY PERSONS, with energy, grace, and intelligence worthy of a better cause, helped make this work possible. Grateful thanks must go first of all to Mr. Paul Green of Chapel Hill, N.C., because the book was really his idea and not mine; to Mr. Herb O'Keef of Raleigh, N.C., who first directed my attention to most of these cases; and to Mr. Jonathan Daniels, publisher of the *Raleigh News and Observer*, who gave ready permission to use much material which had previously appeared in his newspaper.

Several helpful gentlemen made available their special knowledge of individual cases, in particular the Hon. Lindsay Warren, the Hon. Hallett S. Ward, and Mr. John Bragaw of Washington, N.C., and Mr. R. F. Jarrett of Winter Haven, Fla.

Head Librarian Charles Rush and Assistant Librarian O. V. Cook of the University of North Carolina Library, with their able assistants, brought to my attention a great amount of valuable source material and provided quarters in which it could be studied and evaluated.

Advice, information, and references as to various aspects of several cases were generously given by Dr. J. G. de Roulhac Hamilton and Mr. George F. Scheer of Chapel Hill, N.C.; Mr. John R. Peacock of High Point, N.C.; and Mr. J. D. Fitz of Morganton, N.C.

No comprehensive bibliography will be attempted here. Material came from contemporary newspapers, records of courts, letters and family recollections, and various works of local history. Several special notices of some of the cases may interest the reader.

The Trial of Mrs. Ann K. Simpson, Charged With the Murder of Her Husband, Alexander C. Simpson, by Poisoning With Arsenic. . . . New York and Fayetteville, N.C., 1851. A painstaking and totally dispassionate account of the indictment, trial, attorneys' pleas, and verdict of the jury. It bears the notation, *Reported by William H. Haigh.*

Trial of the Rev. George W. Carawan, Baptist Preacher, For the Murder of Clement Lassiter, Schoolmaster, Before the Superior Court of Law of Beaufort County, North Carolina, Fall Term, 1853. n. p., n. d. Comprehensive and fiercely anti-Carawan, including not only a report of the trial but luridly denunciatory material on Carawan's life and character. No author is given, but it is supposed to have been written by a member of the Washington, N.C., bar.

The Muddy Creek Murder Mystery, n. p., n. d. Probably printed from newspaper accounts in Winston-Salem, shortly after the trial in 1915. It includes portraits of the principals and ends on a highly moralistic note.

Evidence of the Beasley-Harrison Kidnapping Case. Elizabeth City, N.C., n. d. (probably 1907). Apparently made up of local newspaper accounts, complete with headlines, but fully covering testimony as given in court. Anonymous.

Naomi Wise, or the Wrongs of a Beautiful Girl. . . . Pinnacle, N.C., n. d. (probably 1884). Several editions of this romantic account by Braxton Craven have been published. Very little about Naomi Wise can be found elsewhere.

Murder and Mystery: History of the Life and Death of John W. Stephens, State Senator of North Carolina from Caswell County, by A. J. Stedman of Danbury, N.C. Greensboro, N.C., 1870. Stedman did not like Stephens and perhaps did not like the method of his murder.

Official Court Record of the Trial, Conviction and Execution of Francis Silvers (sic) *First Woman Hanged in N.C.,* by Clifton K. Avery. n. p., n. d., probably Morganton, N.C., 1952. Mr. Avery studied the Silver case and wrote several accounts for the Morganton *News-Herald.* He includes all court records extant, with penetrating observations upon them.